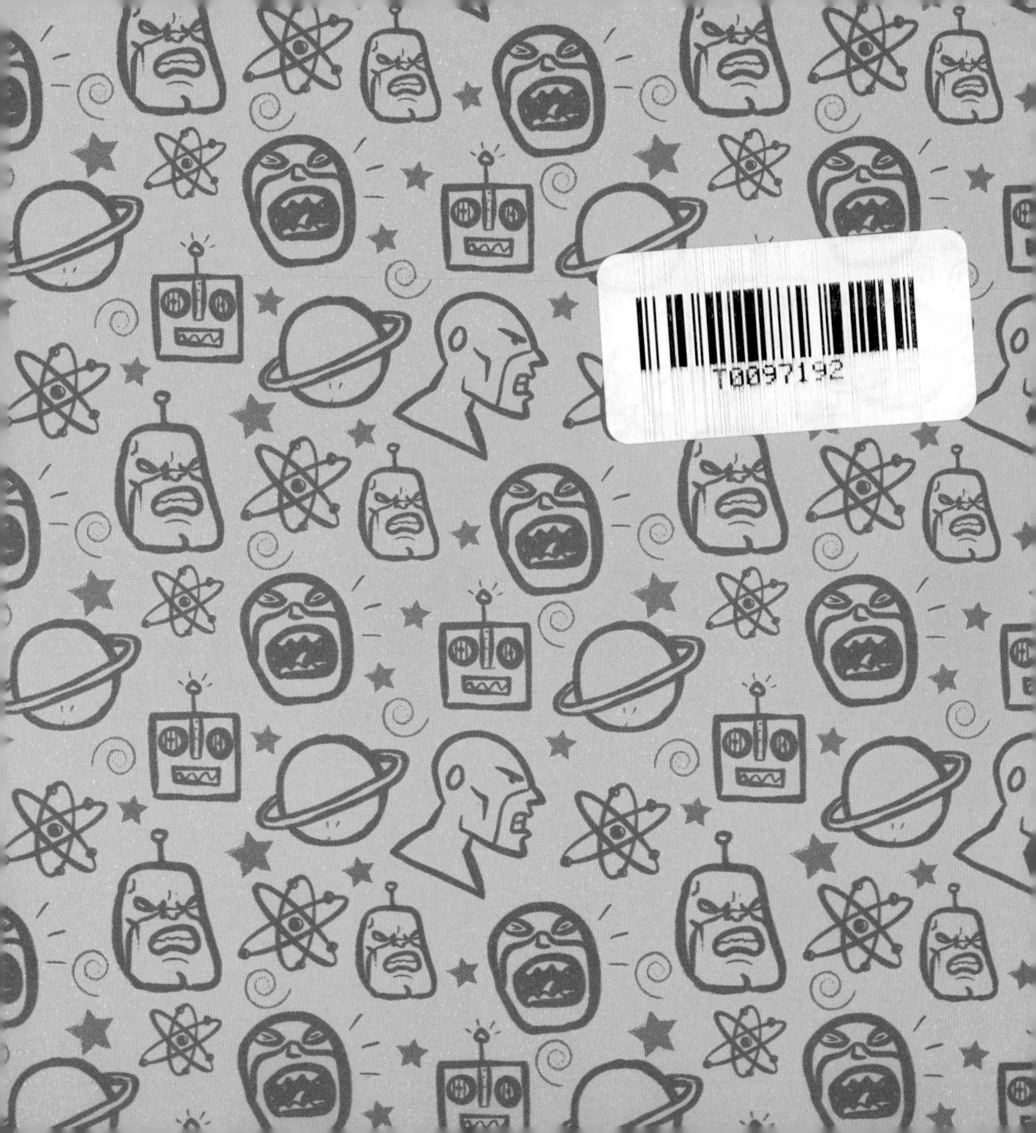

Published by Ice House Books

Copyright © 2019 Ice House Books

Written by Dan Whitehead
Illustrated by Pedro Demetriou
Designed by Rhys Kitson

Ice House Books is an imprint of Half Moon Bay Limited
The Ice House, 124 Walcot Street, Bath, BA1 5BG
www.icehousebooks.co.uk

ISBN 978-1-912867-28-8

Printed in China

SELF-HELP FOR SUPERHEROES

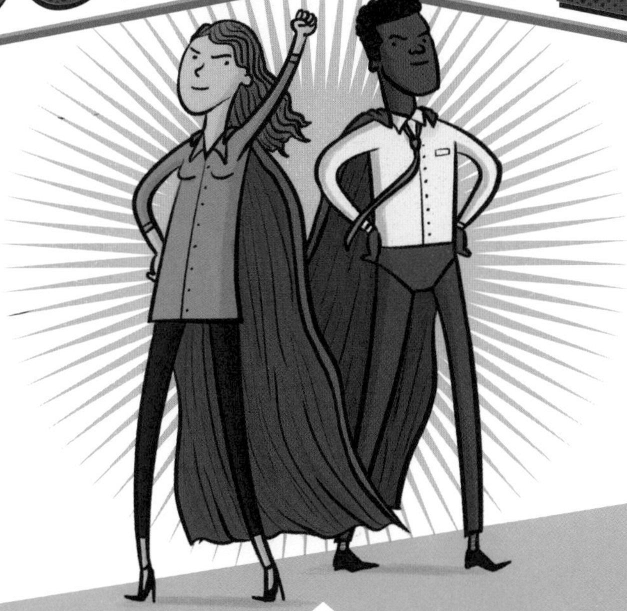

ICE HOUSE BOOKS

SO YOU THINK YOU'RE A SUPERHERO?

Lets make sure...

DEFINITELY A SUPERPOWER

- FLIGHT ○
- INVULNERABILITY ○
- HEAT RAYS ○
- X-RAY VISION ○
- INVISIBILITY ○
- FREEZE BREATH ○
- SUPER SPEED ○

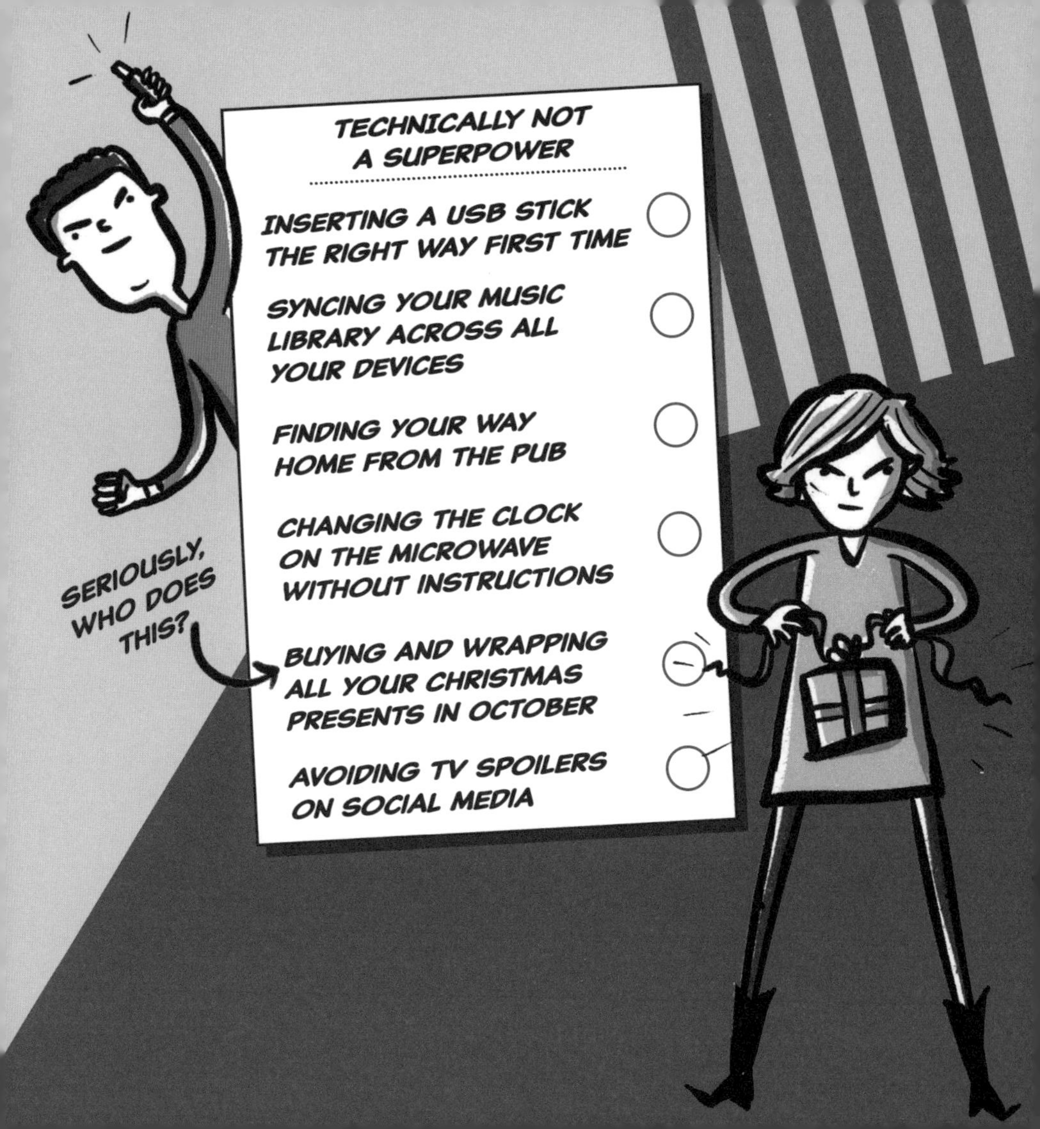
TECHNICALLY NOT A SUPERPOWER
INSERTING A USB STICK THE RIGHT WAY FIRST TIME
SYNCING YOUR MUSIC LIBRARY ACROSS ALL YOUR DEVICES
FINDING YOUR WAY HOME FROM THE PUB
CHANGING THE CLOCK ON THE MICROWAVE WITHOUT INSTRUCTIONS
SERIOUSLY, WHO DOES THIS?
BUYING AND WRAPPING ALL YOUR CHRISTMAS PRESENTS IN OCTOBER
AVOIDING TV SPOILERS ON SOCIAL MEDIA

BORN THIS WAY

Some people gain their superpowers, but others are born with them. Check and see if any of these apply...

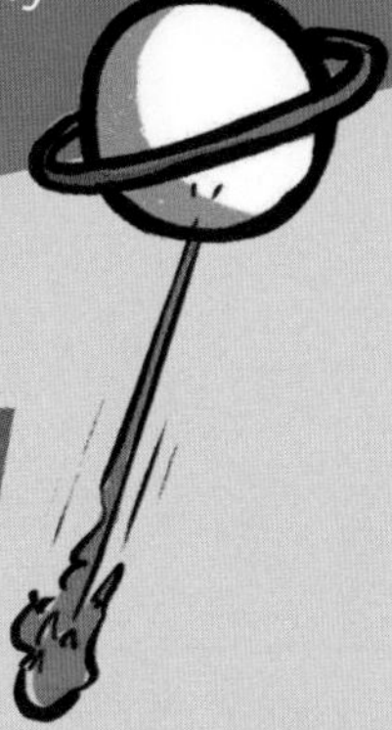

IS YOUR EARLIEST MEMORY BEING BLASTED AWAY FROM A DYING STAR? ☐

DID YOU GET INTO TROUBLE FOR SHOPLIFTING BY LITERALLY LIFTING THE ENTIRE SHOP? ☐

DID YOUR COT RESEMBLE AN ALIEN ESCAPE POD? ☐

DO EITHER OF YOUR PARENTS SHARE THEIR NAME WITH A MAJOR MYTHOLOGICAL FIGURE? ☐

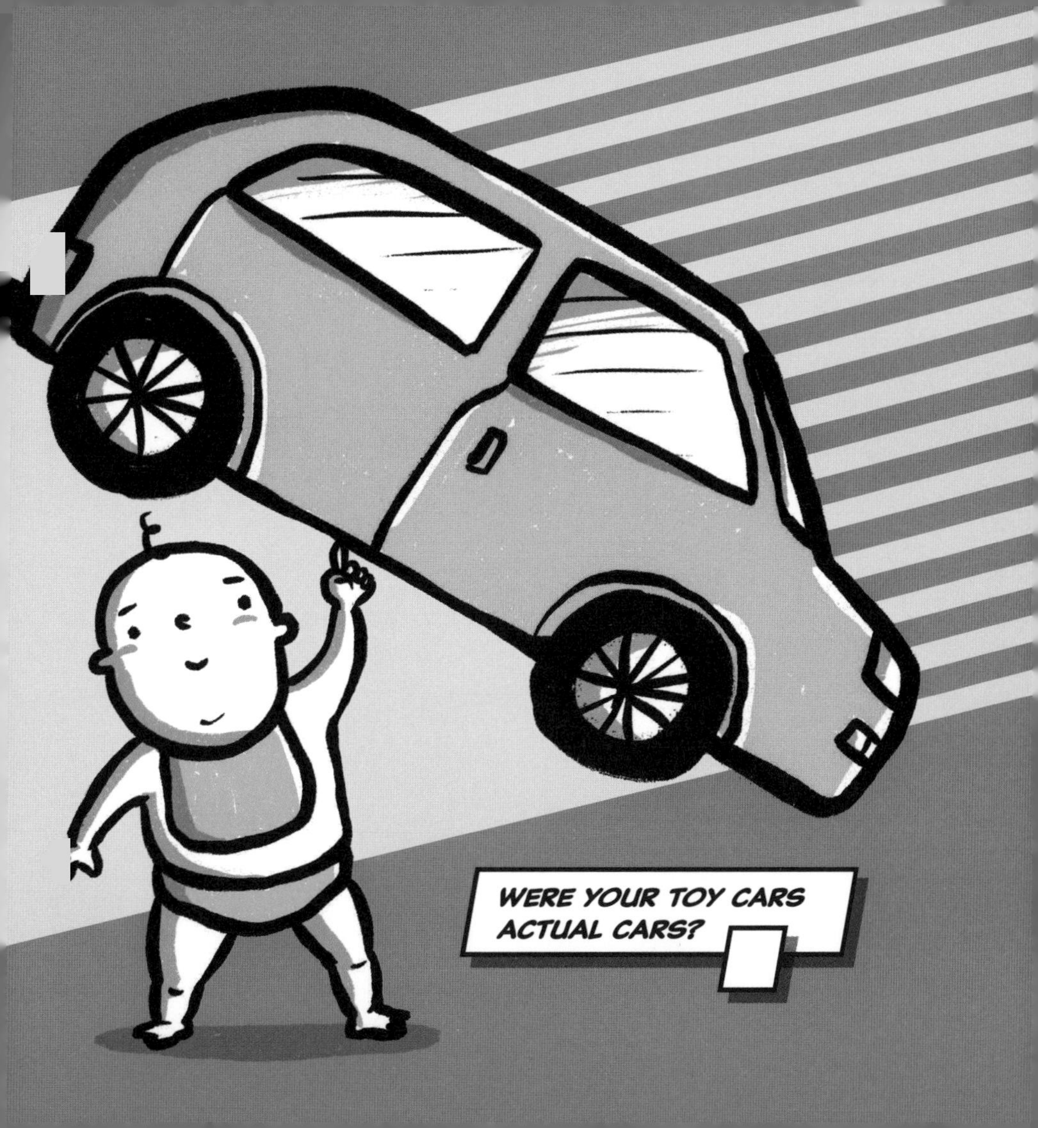
WERE YOUR TOY CARS
ACTUAL CARS?

THE MIGHTY ATOM

If you weren't born super, don't panic! You may have got your powers from atomic radiation instead. It's a scientific fact that radioactive animals pass on their abilities when they bite you. Just try to make sure it's a cool animal...

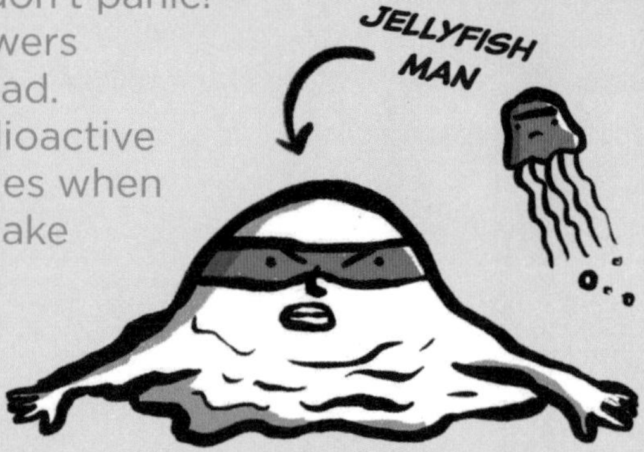
JELLYFISH MAN

ATOMIC EXPLOSIONS ARE ALSO A GOOD SOURCE OF SUPERPOWER – THOUGH THE RESULTS ARE HIT AND MISS.

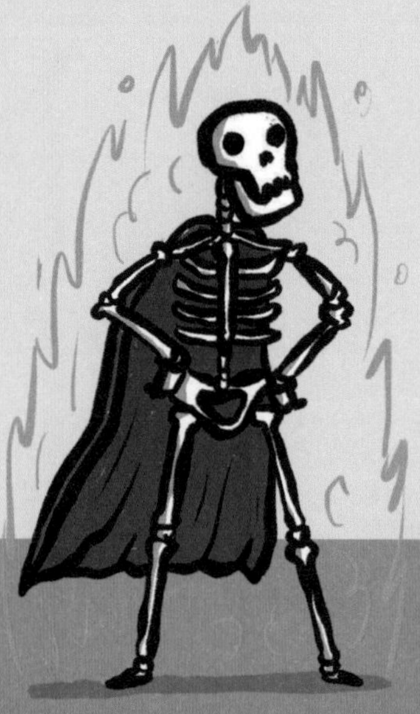

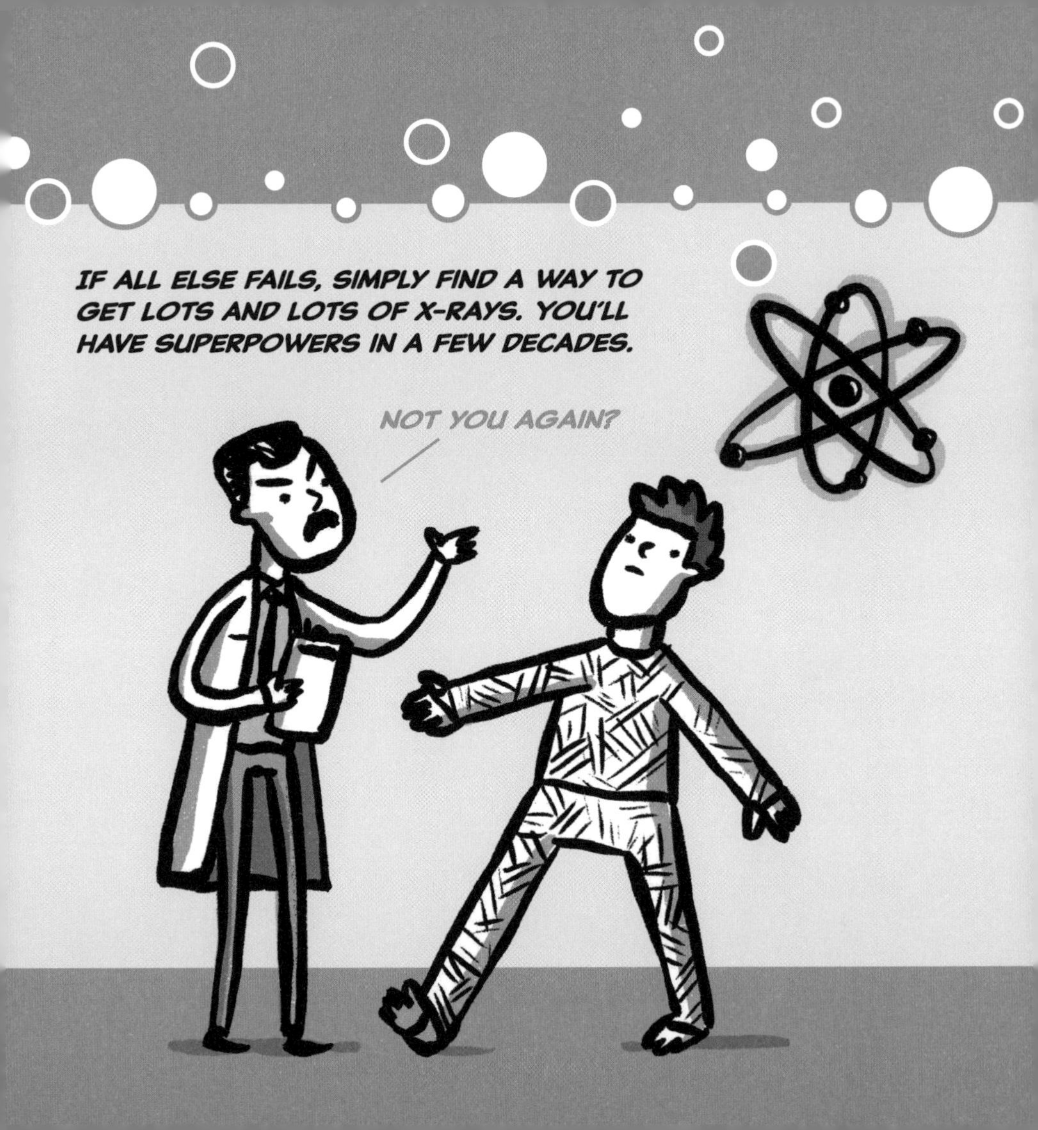
IF ALL ELSE FAILS, SIMPLY FIND A WAY TO GET LOTS AND LOTS OF X-RAYS. YOU'LL HAVE SUPERPOWERS IN A FEW DECADES.
NOT YOU AGAIN?

NO POWERS? NO PROBLEM?

What's that? You don't actually have any superpowers? That's OK! Plenty of famous heroes have managed to have incredibly successful crimefighting careers thanks to technology and gadgets – and so can you!

IMPORTANT NOTE!

THIS APPROACH ONLY WORKS IF YOU'RE A BILLIONAIRE GENIUS WITH LOTS OF TIME ON YOUR HANDS. IF YOU'RE ON A BUDGET, YOU MAY STRUGGLE!

GRAPPLING HOOKS ARE A GADGET HERO'S BEST FRIEND! BE SURE TO PRACTISE BEFORE HEADING OUT ON PATROL FOR THE FIRST TIME!

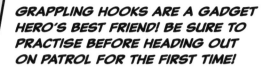

PLEASE STOP

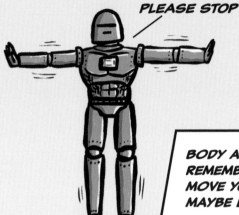

BODY ARMOUR IS VITAL! JUST REMEMBER THAT YOU WILL NEED TO MOVE YOUR ARMS AND LEGS, AND MAYBE EVEN TURN YOUR HEAD!

IT'S GOOD TO BE PREPARED, BUT DON'T GET CARRIED AWAY. SAY "YES" TO SMOKE BOMBS, BUT "NO" TO MUTANT PARROT REPELLENT*.

*UNLESS YOU'RE FIGHTING MUTANT PARROTS, OBVIOUSLY.

SUPER SPEED

A BEGINNER'S GUIDE

Super speed can be super useful, but it also has its downsides.
Be sure you can super-walk before you super-run...

PRO
YOU'LL NEVER MISS ANOTHER TRAIN.
IN FACT, YOU'LL NEVER NEED TO
CATCH THE TRAIN AGAIN!

CON
HUMAN FACES DO NOT HAVE WINDSCREEN WIPERS. WEAR GOGGLES UNLESS YOU FANCY AN INSECT FACIAL.

PRO
YOU'LL ALWAYS GET TO THE DOOR IN TIME WHEN A DELIVERY ARRIVES WHILE YOU'RE IN THE SHOWER.

CON
THOSE OFF-BRAND TRAINERS WON'T LAST LONG AT MACH 5. INVEST IN STURDY FOOTWEAR AND BLISTER CREAM.

THE DOS AND DON'TS OF
FLYING

In your face, gravity! You have the power to soar majestically above the common herd, but it doesn't take much to bring you down to earth...

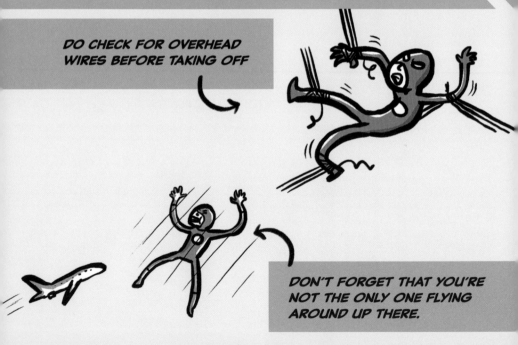

DO CHECK FOR OVERHEAD WIRES BEFORE TAKING OFF

DON'T FORGET THAT YOU'RE NOT THE ONLY ONE FLYING AROUND UP THERE.

DO THINK ABOUT HOW YOUR COSTUME WILL LOOK FROM BELOW. THIS IS WHY SO MANY SUPERHEROES HAVE THEIR UNDERWEAR ON THE OUTSIDE.

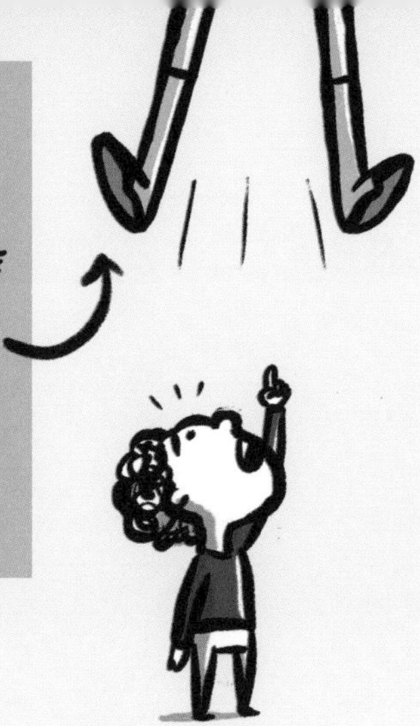

DON'T GET INTO A TERRITORIAL DISPUTE WITH PIGEONS. SERIOUSLY. THEY WILL MESS YOU UP.

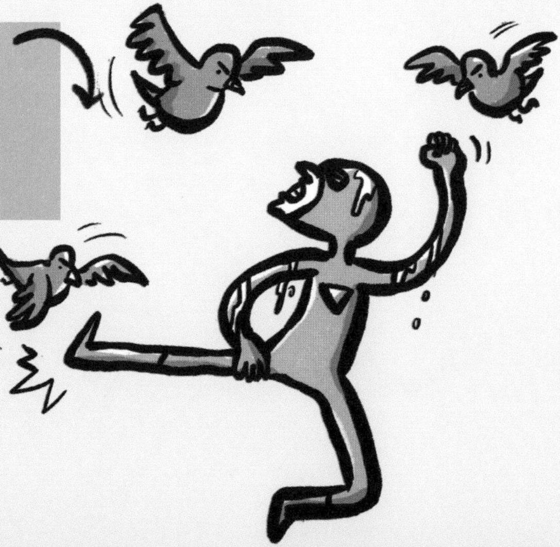

LIVING WITH

SUPER STRENGTH

You're the strongest person on Earth, but while mighty muscles are useful when saving the world, they can be a problem in day-to-day life...

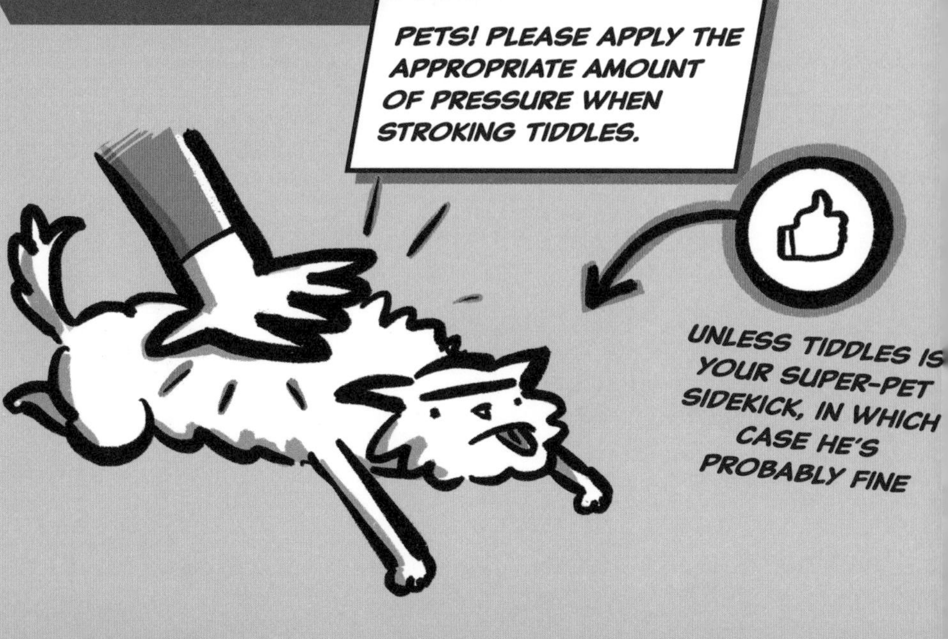
PETS! PLEASE APPLY THE APPROPRIATE AMOUNT OF PRESSURE WHEN STROKING TIDDLES.
UNLESS TIDDLES IS YOUR SUPER-PET SIDEKICK, IN WHICH CASE HE'S PROBABLY FINE

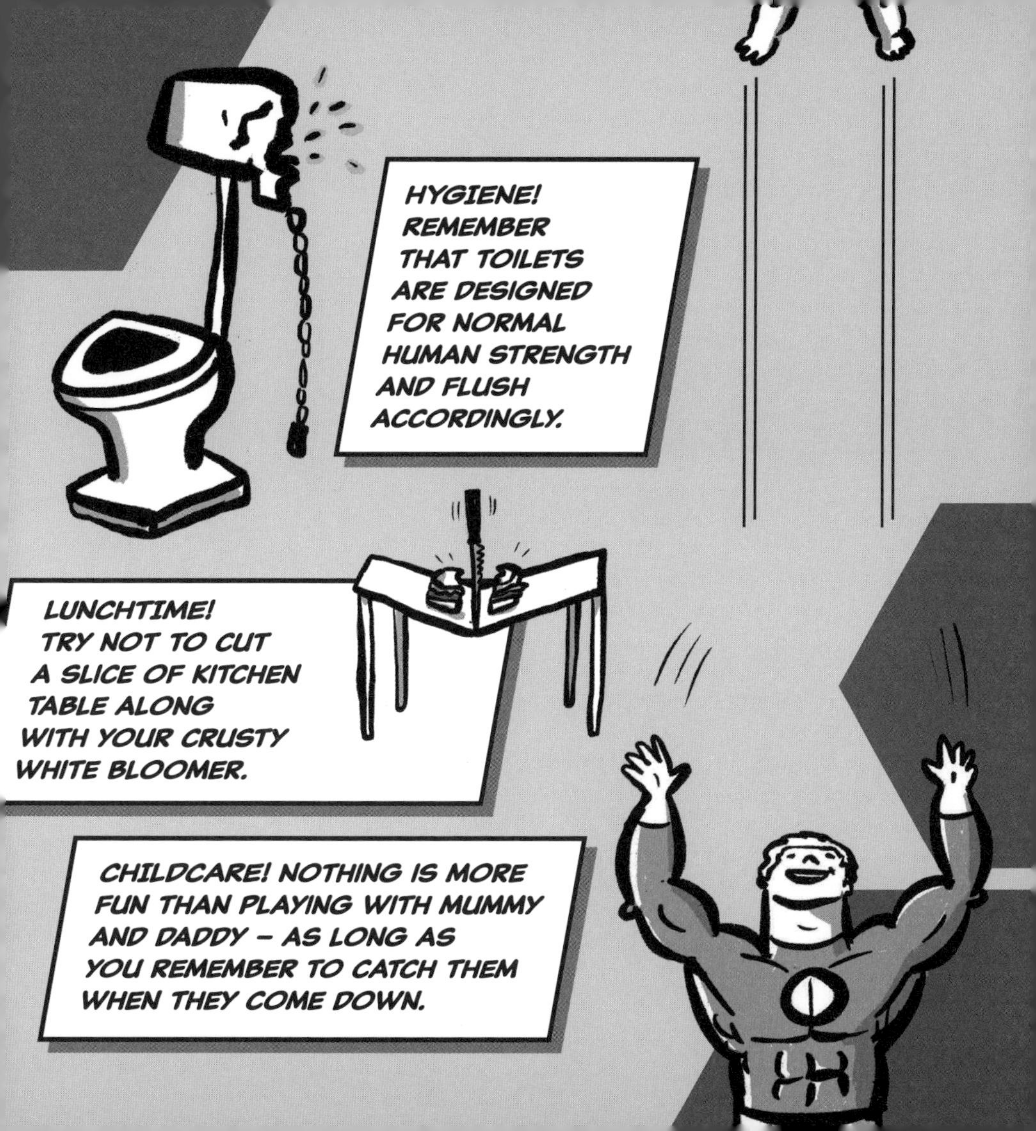
HYGIENE! REMEMBER THAT TOILETS ARE DESIGNED FOR NORMAL HUMAN STRENGTH AND FLUSH ACCORDINGLY.
LUNCHTIME! TRY NOT TO CUT A SLICE OF KITCHEN TABLE ALONG WITH YOUR CRUSTY WHITE BLOOMER.
CHILDCARE! NOTHING IS MORE FUN THAN PLAYING WITH MUMMY AND DADDY – AS LONG AS YOU REMEMBER TO CATCH THEM WHEN THEY COME DOWN.

ALTERNATE CAREERS

Before you embark on your new life as a superhero, there's still time to pause and reconsider. Are there other lines of work where your powers could prove useful? **Yes!** And here they are...

PIZZA DELIVERY! PIPING HOT DEEP PAN DIRECT TO YOUR DOOR IN 30 SECONDS OR LESS!

HAIRDRESSER! SUPER-BREATH GIVES A BETTER BLOW-DRY THAN ANY HAIRDRYER!

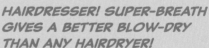

WINDOW CLEANER! WHO NEEDS TO WASTE MONEY ON LADDERS WHEN YOU CAN FLY?

BOUNCER! WHEN YOU HAVE THE STRENGTH OF TEN MEN, NOBODY IS GETTING IN THE CLUB WEARING TRAINERS!

AIRPORT SECURITY! X-RAY VISION MAKES SNOOPING THROUGH SUITCASES A DODDLE!

PROTECTING YOUR SECRET IDENTITY

Do you have everything you need to keep your heroics under wraps?

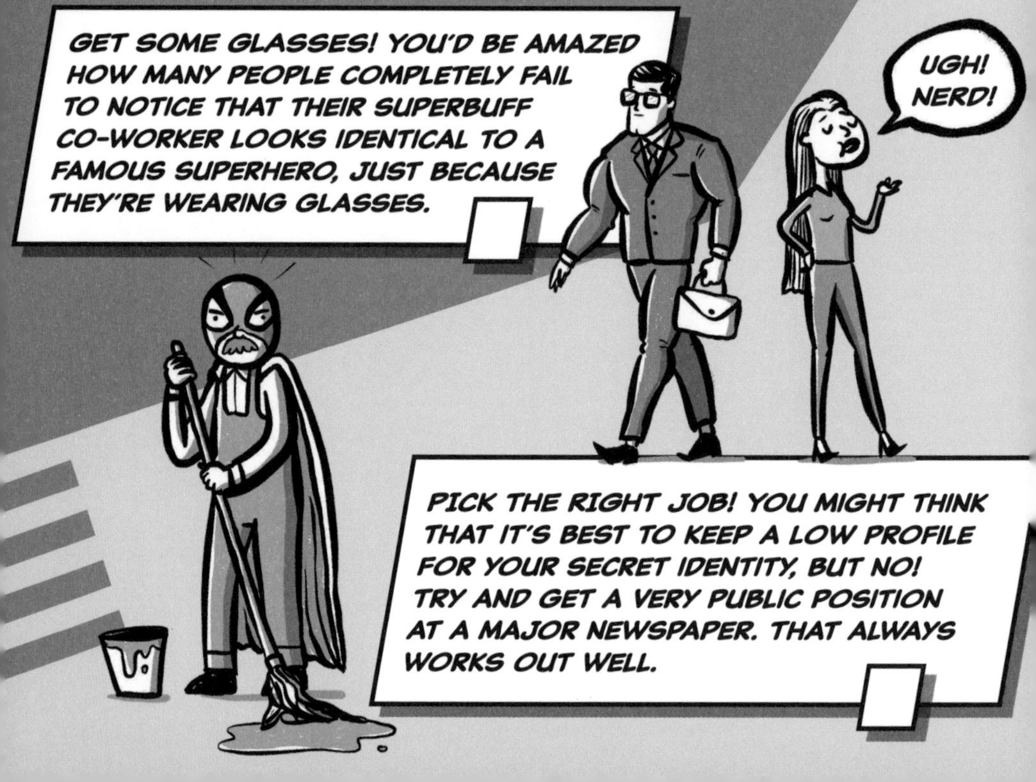

GET SOME GLASSES! YOU'D BE AMAZED HOW MANY PEOPLE COMPLETELY FAIL TO NOTICE THAT THEIR SUPERBUFF CO-WORKER LOOKS IDENTICAL TO A FAMOUS SUPERHERO, JUST BECAUSE THEY'RE WEARING GLASSES.
UGH! NERD!
PICK THE RIGHT JOB! YOU MIGHT THINK THAT IT'S BEST TO KEEP A LOW PROFILE FOR YOUR SECRET IDENTITY, BUT NO! TRY AND GET A VERY PUBLIC POSITION AT A MAJOR NEWSPAPER. THAT ALWAYS WORKS OUT WELL.

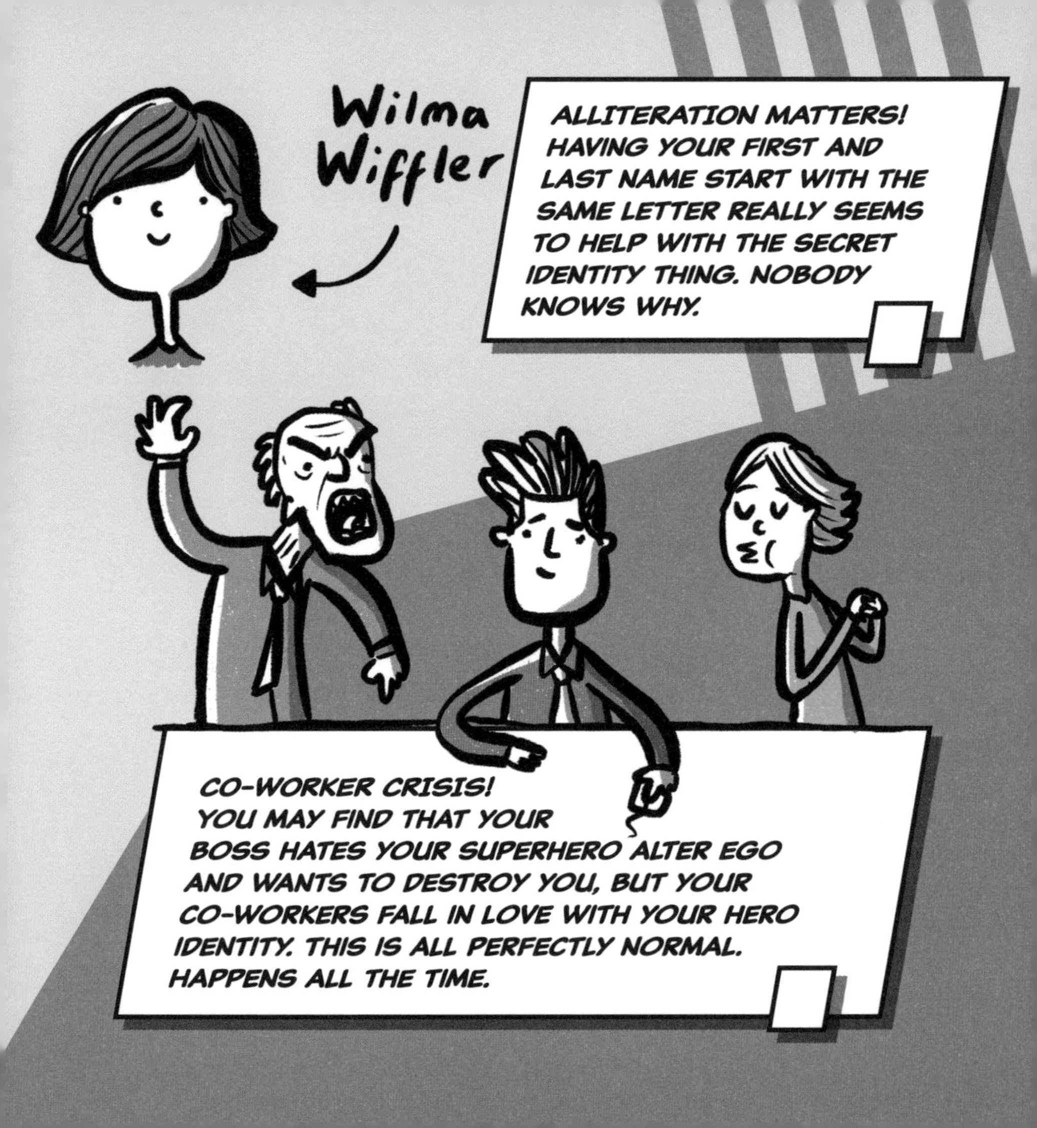
Wilma Wiffler
ALLITERATION MATTERS! HAVING YOUR FIRST AND LAST NAME START WITH THE SAME LETTER REALLY SEEMS TO HELP WITH THE SECRET IDENTITY THING. NOBODY KNOWS WHY.
CO-WORKER CRISIS! YOU MAY FIND THAT YOUR BOSS HATES YOUR SUPERHERO ALTER EGO AND WANTS TO DESTROY YOU, BUT YOUR CO-WORKERS FALL IN LOVE WITH YOUR HERO IDENTITY. THIS IS ALL PERFECTLY NORMAL. HAPPENS ALL THE TIME.

BEHIND THE MASK

Important things to consider when choosing a mask to hide your identity...

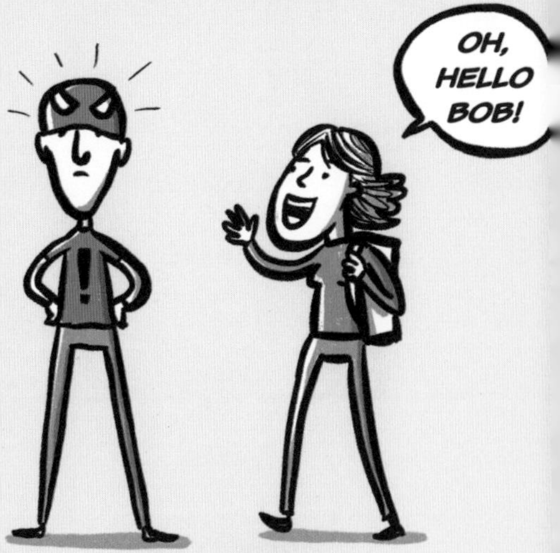
OH, HELLO BOB!

DO MAKE SURE THE MASK IS LARGE ENOUGH TO ACTUALLY DISGUISE YOUR FACE.

DON'T TRY TO SAVE MONEY BY BUYING ONE AT THE LOCAL FANCY DRESS SHOP.

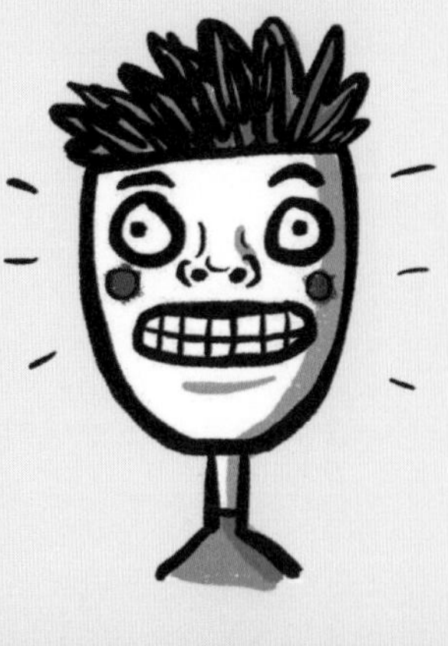

DO THINK ABOUT
PRACTICAL ISSUES
– LIKE VISIBILITY.

DON'T PANIC IF YOU
CAN'T FIND A MASK
– JUST IMPROVISE!

TO CAPE OR NOT TO CAPE

These iconic costume items make for a flamboyant entrance, but do have their downsides...

TOP TIP!

AN OLD BED SHEET WORKS AS A CAPE REPLACEMENT FOR THE SUPERHERO ON A BUDGET. JUST MAKE SURE YOU WASH IT FIRST.

SIZE MATTERS!

GET THE TAPE MEASURE OUT BEFORE YOU GET TO WORK, OR YOU COULD END UP LOOKING VERY SILLY.

BE BUSINESS SMART!

A MAJESTIC FLOWING CAPE IS PRIME ADVERTISING REAL ESTATE – DON'T BE ASHAMED TO PUT IT TO USE!

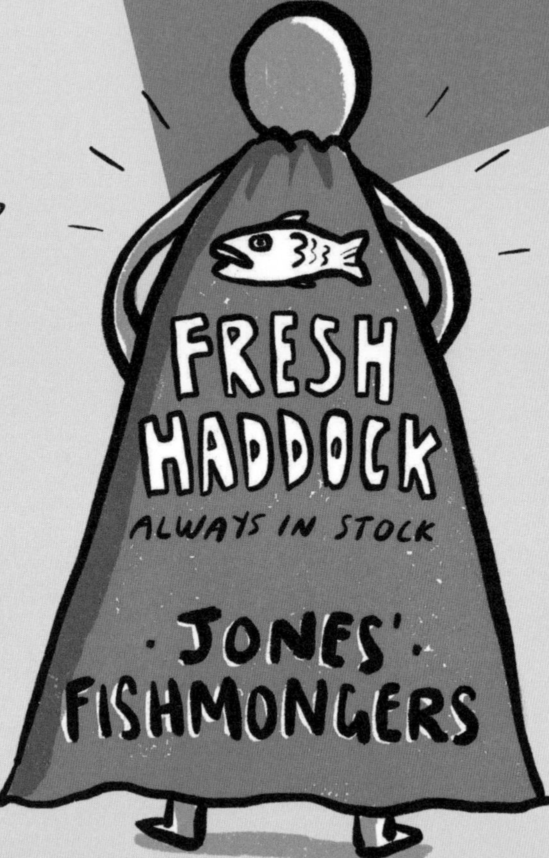

FRESH HADDOCK
ALWAYS IN STOCK
JONES'
FISHMONGERS

MORE THAN JUST FASHION!

IT CAN GET PRETTY CHILLY ON THOSE WINDSWEPT ROOFTOPS AT NIGHT. AN EXTRA THICK SNUGGLY CAPE CAN MAKE ALL THE DIFFERENCE!

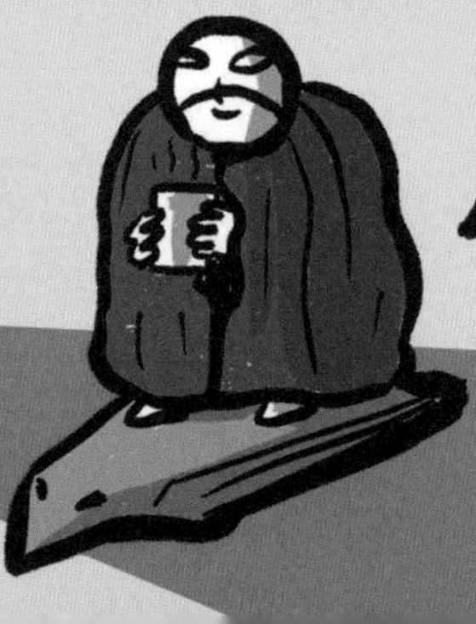

QUICK CHANGE

Every superhero needs to be able to burst into action at a moment's notice but finding the right place to change costume isn't easy.

PHONE BOX! A CLASSIC, BUT SADLY NO LONGER VIABLE. MOST PHONE BOXES ARE SHATTERED HUSKS THESE DAYS, AND PRIVACY IS NOT GUARANTEED.

SPRAY TAN BOOTH! THE PERFECT SIZE, BUT THERE IS A CONSIDERABLE RISK OF COMING OUT BRIGHT ORANGE. RECOMMENDED FOR CARROT-THEMED HEROES ONLY.

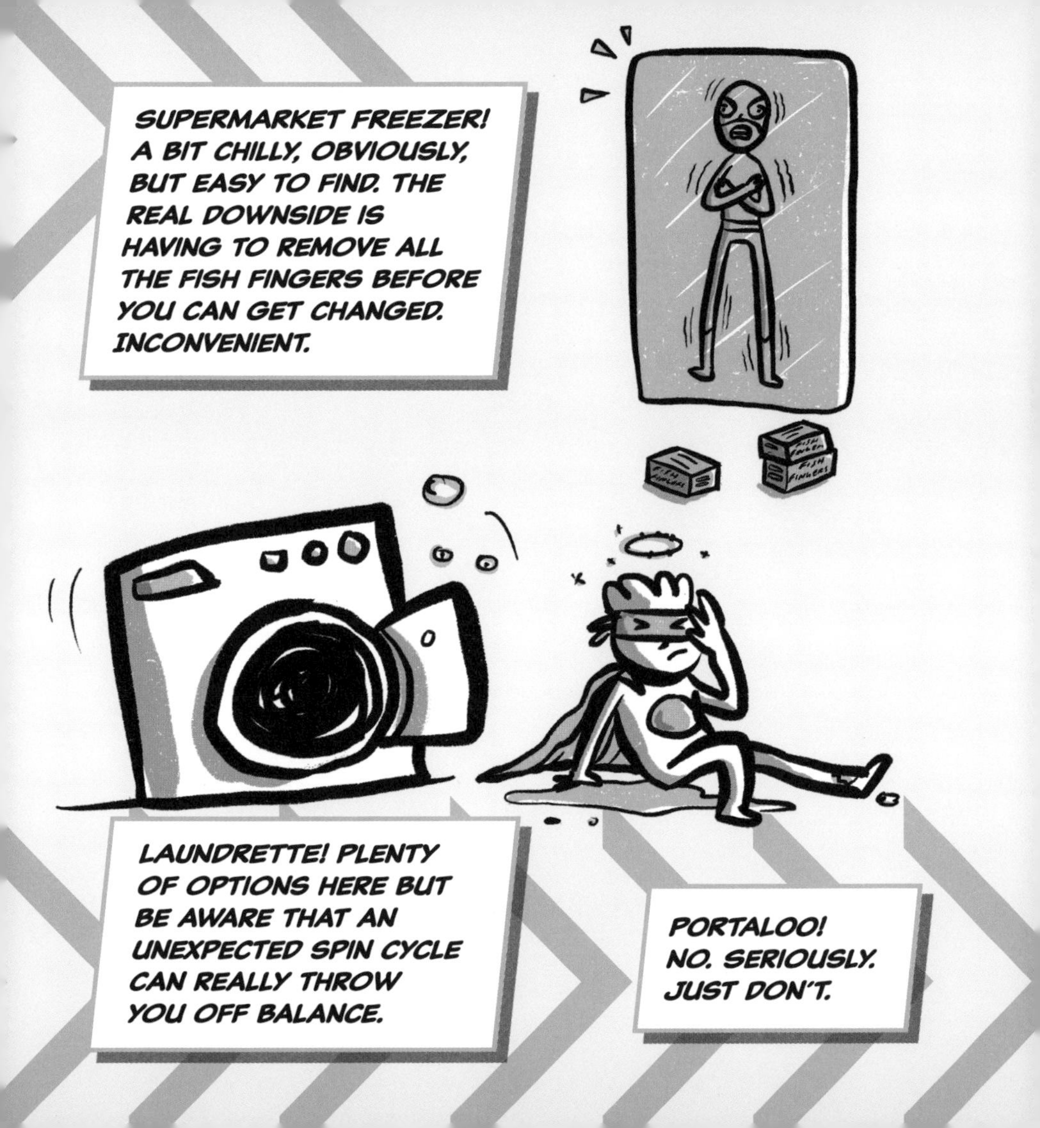
SUPERMARKET FREEZER! A BIT CHILLY, OBVIOUSLY, BUT EASY TO FIND. THE REAL DOWNSIDE IS HAVING TO REMOVE ALL THE FISH FINGERS BEFORE YOU CAN GET CHANGED. INCONVENIENT.
FISH FINGERS
FISH FINGERS
FISH FINGERS
LAUNDRETTE! PLENTY OF OPTIONS HERE BUT BE AWARE THAT AN UNEXPECTED SPIN CYCLE CAN REALLY THROW YOU OFF BALANCE.
PORTALOO! NO. SERIOUSLY. JUST DON'T.

THE PERFECT SUPERHERO NAME

You could put a lot of thought into this – or you could just use this foolproof system. Simply pick one word from each section. Job done!

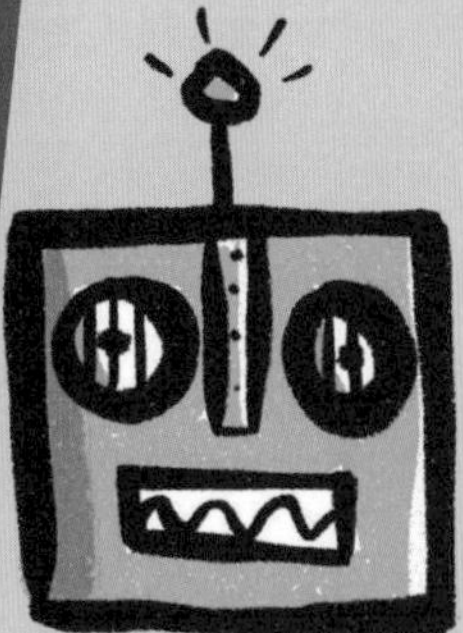

GORGEOUS
GROOVY
INCOHERENT
BEEFY
BABBLING
UNBELIEVABLE
IMPOSSIBLE
FABULOUS
IMPECCABLE
ASTONISHING
TERRIFYING
WONDERFUL
SAUCY
SWOLLEN
LOVABLE
MAJESTIC
AMAZING

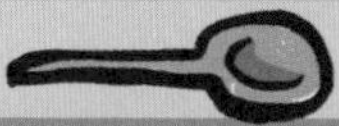

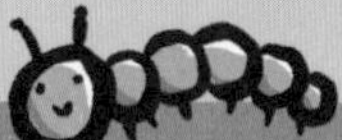

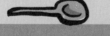

PHOTOCOPIER
COFFEE
WOODPECKER
CARPET
WOMBAT
SKELETON
FLATULENT
DOUGHNUT
LOBSTER
PORRIDGE
PUMPKIN
BOBBLE
CUTLERY
SAUSAGE
HAT
MICROWAVE
SPAGHETTI
TRUMPET
UPHOLSTERY
CATERPILLAR
NETTLE

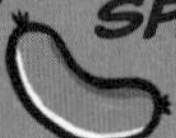

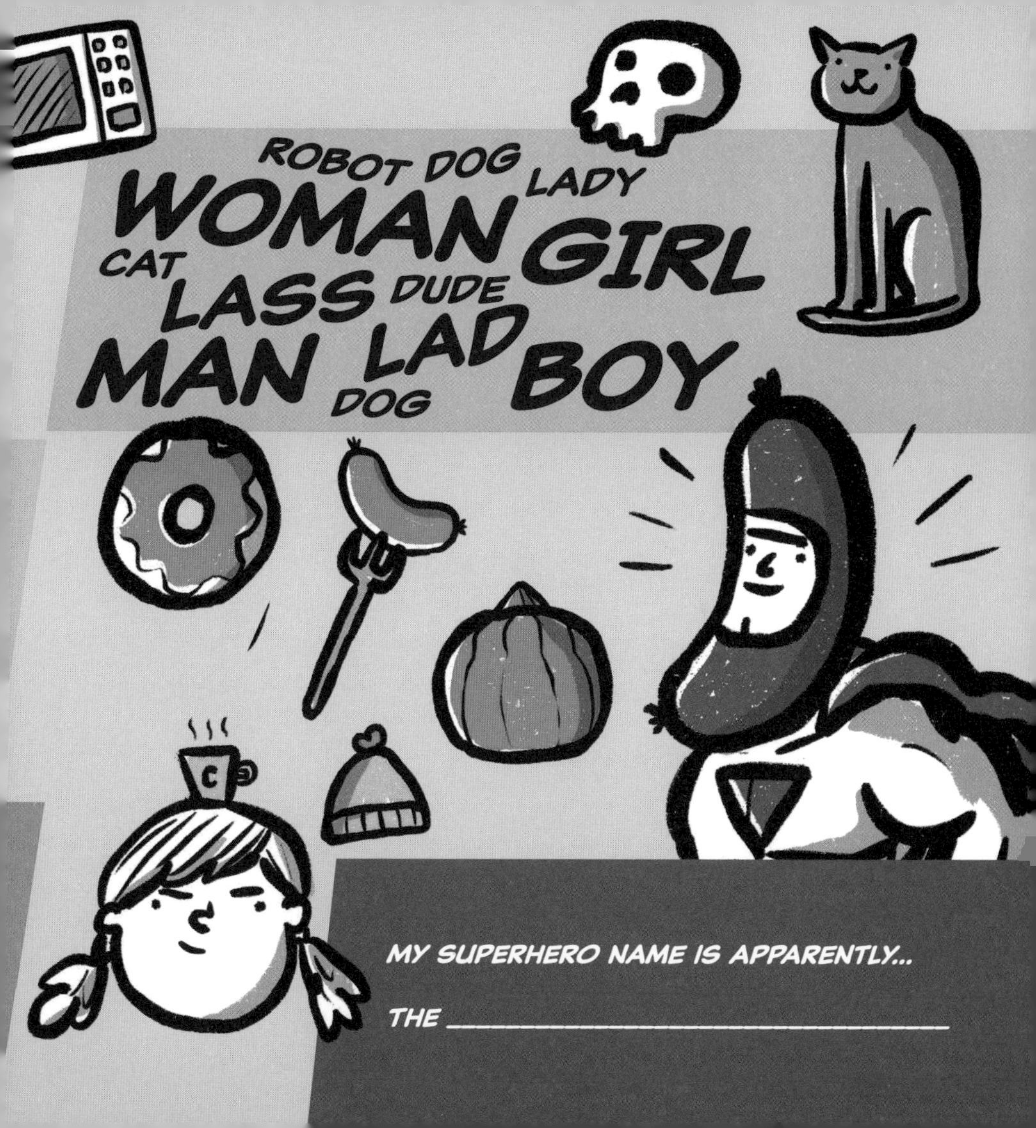
ROBOT DOG
LADY
WOMAN
GIRL
CAT
LASS
DUDE
MAN
LAD
BOY
DOG
MY SUPERHERO NAME IS APPARENTLY...
THE ____________________________

GETTING AROUND

Can't fly? No super-speed? You're going to need a sweet superhero ride!

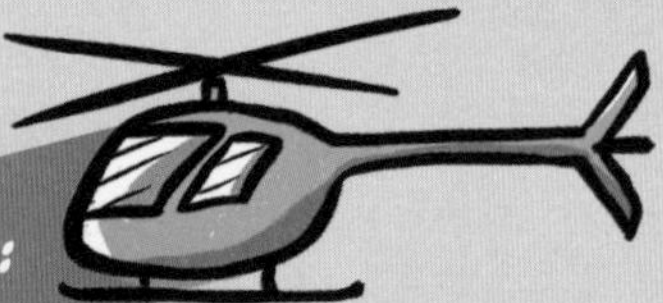

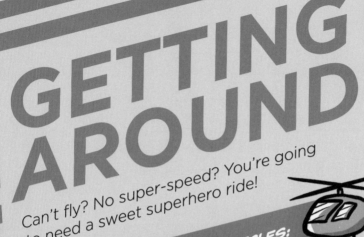

ACCEPTABLE SUPERHERO VEHICLES:

- SOUPED-UP SPORTS CAR
- HEAVILY ARMED TANK
- STATE-OF-THE-ART HELICOPTER
- COMBINATION SPEEDBOAT-SUBMARINE
- SUPERSONIC JET PLANE

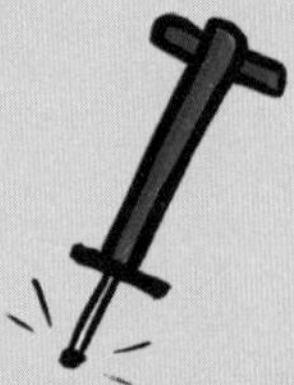

UNACCEPTABLE SUPERHERO VEHICLES:

- ICE-CREAM VAN
- FOOT SCOOTER
- MINIBUS
- TRACTOR
- TRICYCLE
- POGO STICK

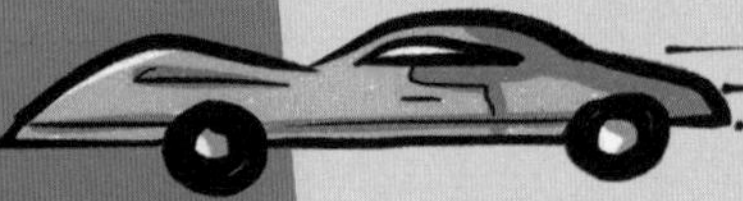

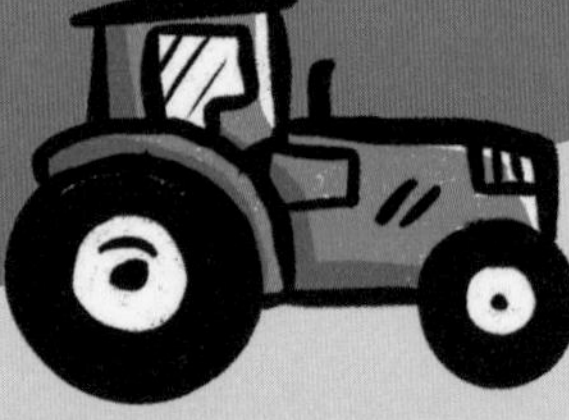

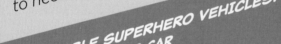

SPECIAL NOTE

AN ACTUAL HOVERBOARD – A BOARD THAT DEFIES GRAVITY – IS AN EXCELLENT SUPERHERO MODE OF TRANSPORT.

THOSE PLASTIC PLANKS WITH TWO WHEELS YOU GET FROM THE KNOCK-OFF ELECTRONICS STALL IN THE MARKET? NOPE. NOT THE SAME THING.

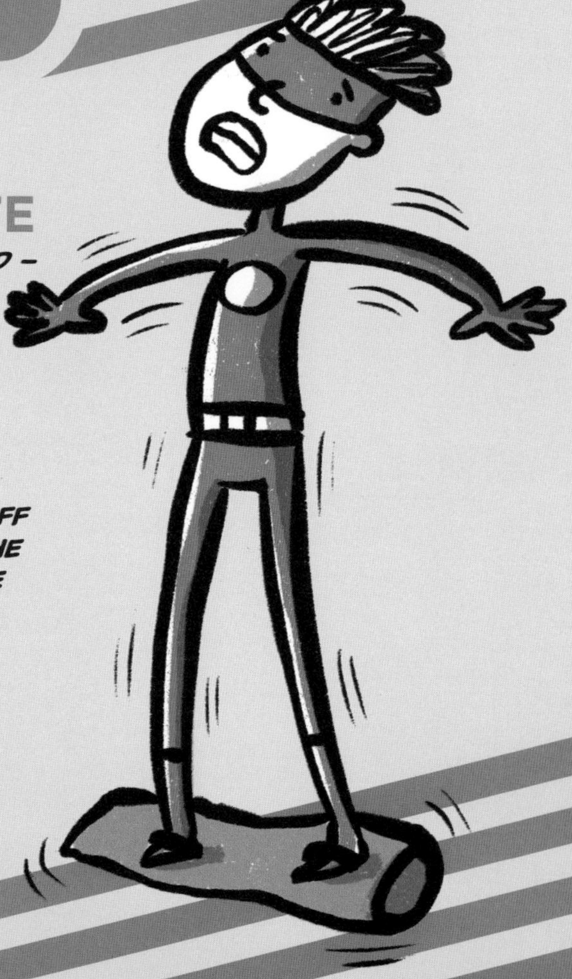

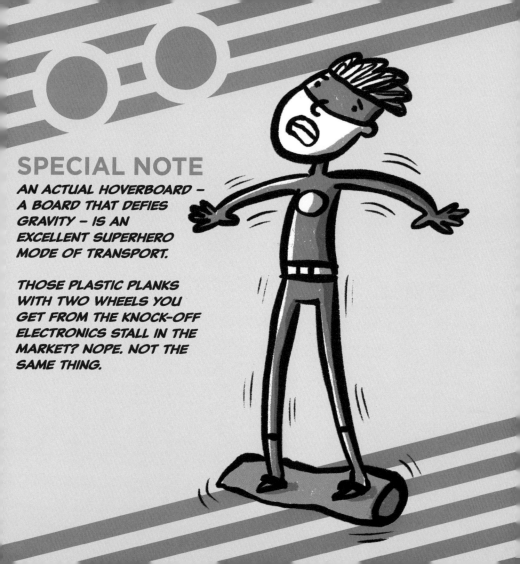

SECRET HQ MAKEOVER

Once you're an established crimefighter you're going to need a base of operations – and it needs to be awesome!

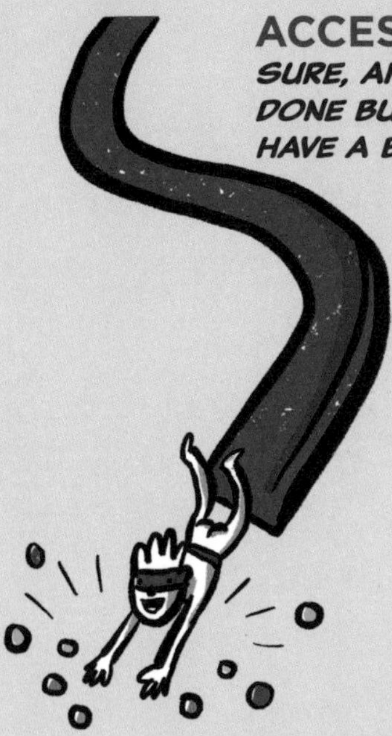

ACCESS

SURE, AN ELEVATOR GETS THE JOB DONE BUT IT'S MUCH MORE FUN TO HAVE A BENDY SLIDE AND BALL POOL.

CRIME COMPUTER

IDEALLY YOU'RE GOING TO WANT A SELF-AWARE ARTIFICIAL INTELLIGENCE WITH A SARCASTIC ENGLISH ACCENT TO PLAN YOUR NEXT MOVE, BUT A SECOND-HAND LAPTOP WILL ALSO GET THE JOB DONE.

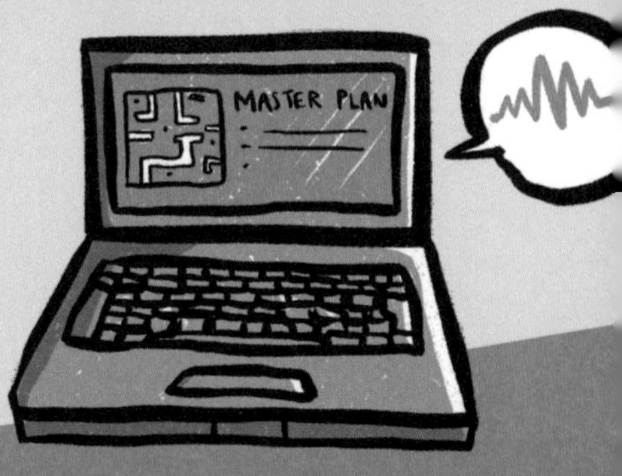
MASTER PLAN

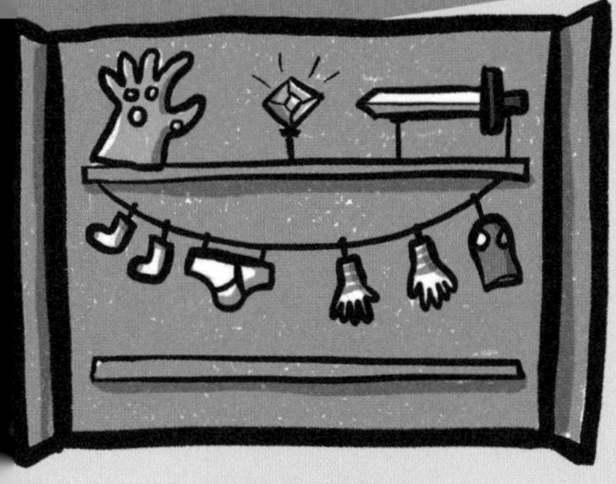

TROPHY ROOM

WHERE ELSE ARE YOU GOING TO STORE THE OUTSIZED PROPS, GADGETS AND WEAPONS YOU CONFISCATE FROM YOUR ENEMIES? ALSO USEFUL AS A PLACE TO HANG YOUR WASHING.

GARAGE

HOME TO ALL YOUR SUPER VEHICLES AND SEVEN BOXES OF RANDOM CABLES AND PLUGS THAT YOU'RE SURE YOU'LL NEED ONE DAY.

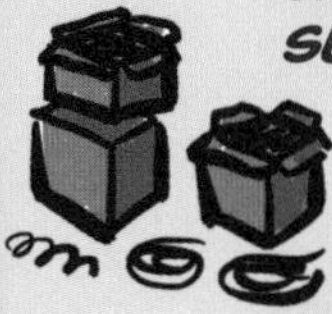

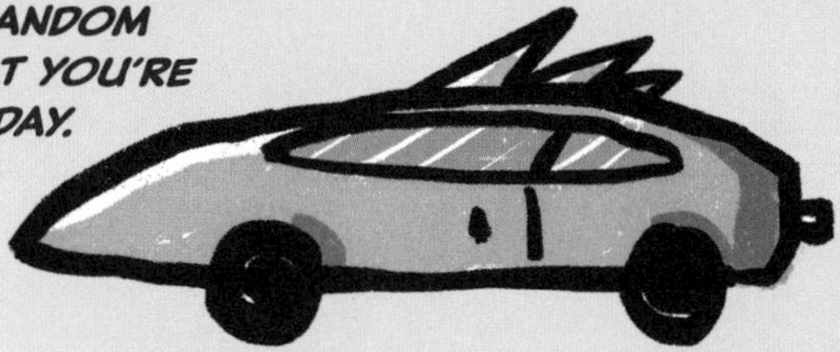

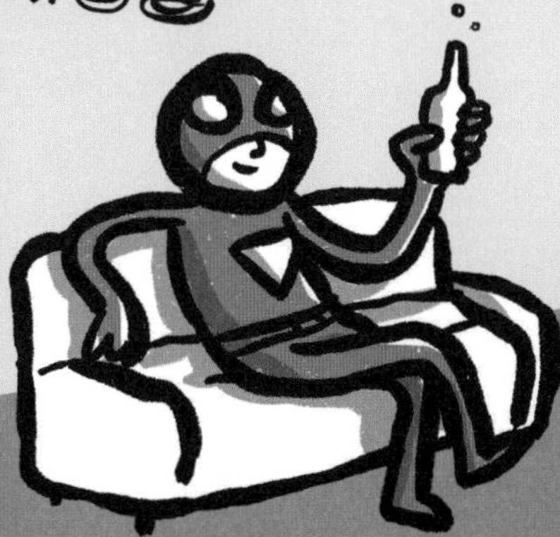

WORKSHOP

AKA THE ROOM WITH A MINI-FRIDGE AND COMFY SOFA FOR SERIOUS CRIME-FIGHTING THINKING TIME.

USE YOUR WORDS

As a superhero your words need to inspire the innocent and terrify the guilty. Please don't get those muddled up.

RULE 1: THERE IS NO SUCH THING AS AN "INSIDE VOICE" FOR SUPERHEROES. EVERYTHING MUST BE SPOKEN AT MAXIMUM BELLOW.

RULE 2: ALWAYS REFER TO CRIMINALS AS "EVILDOERS" AND MEMBERS OF THE PUBLIC AS "CITIZENS".

BONUS TIP:

IF GOING FOR A "DARK WARRIOR OF THE NIGHT" VIBE, YOU'LL NEED TO GROWL CONSTANTLY. NEVER LEAVE HOME WITHOUT SOME THROAT SWEETS. HANDY HINT: FOR THE PERFECT SUPERHERO SLOGAN, JUST CRACK OPEN A FORTUNE COOKIE AND REPLACE ANY NOUNS WITH THE WORD "JUSTICE".

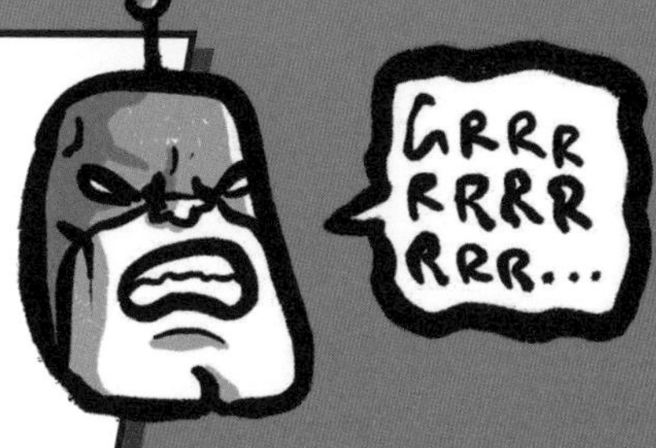
GRRR RRRR RRR...

RULE 3: NEVER USE ORDINARY WORDS. SAY "HALT!" INSTEAD OF "STOP!" OR "VERY WELL!" INSTEAD OF "OK!"

RULE 4: BASICALLY, TALK LIKE YOU'RE AUDITIONING FOR A LOCAL DRAMA SOCIETY SHAKESPEARE SEASON.

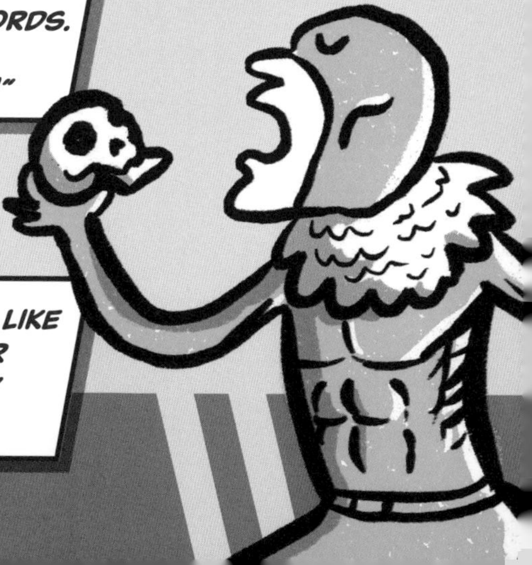

CALL ME, MAYBE

Oh no! A crime is in progress! How will the police summon your crimefighting assistance? Read on...

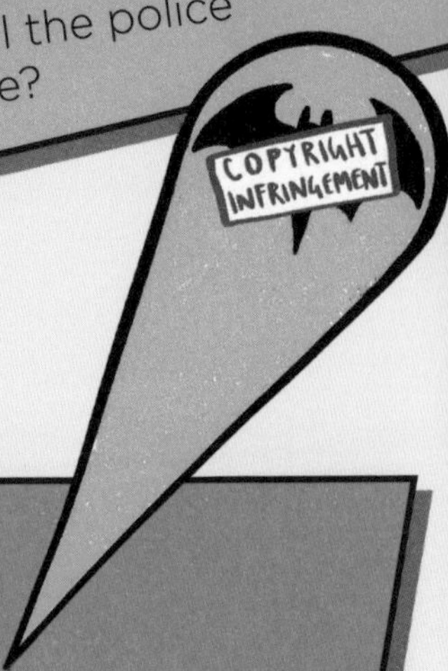
COPYRIGHT
INFRINGEMENT

OPTION 1:
GIANT ROOFTOP SPOTLIGHT
PROS: LOOKS AWESOME, EXCELLENT BRANDING OPPORTUNITY.
CONS: COSTS A FORTUNE, ALREADY BEEN DONE.

OPTION 2:
LARGE KAZOO
PROS: SURPRISINGLY AFFORDABLE, YOU CAN DANCE TO IT.
CONS: REQUIRES A LOT OF BLOWING, SOUNDS LIKE WASPS.

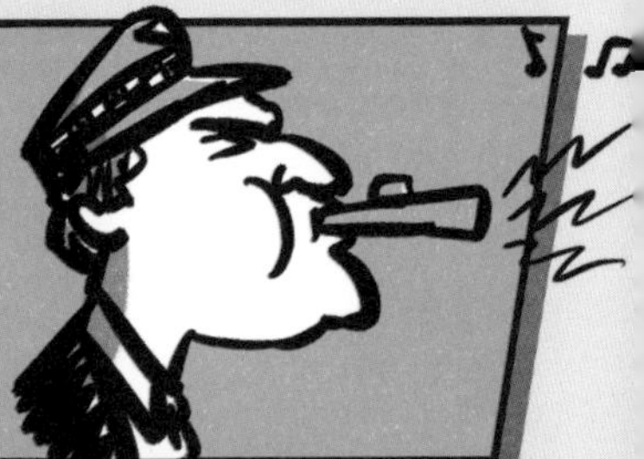

OPTION 3:
YODELLING
PROS: AUDIBLE ACROSS LONG DISTANCES, LEDERHOSEN ARE TOTALLY "IN" THIS SEASON.
CONS: MAY CAUSE AN AVALANCHE. YES, EVEN IN THE BIG CITY.

POLICE

WE NEED YOUR HELP NOW!!

New number, who dis?

OPTION 4:
TEXT MESSAGE
PROS: EVERYONE CAN DO IT, UNLIMITED TEXTS ON A MONTHLY CONTRACT.
CONS: KIND OF BLOWS THE SECRET IDENTITY TO PIECES.

SUPERHERO PR

How to keep the police and press on your side.

COP THIS!

IT'S USEFUL TO HAVE THE LOCAL POLICE CHIEF AS AN ALLY. THIS WILL ALMOST CERTAINLY BE A CRANKY OLD GAL WITH A SENSIBLE HAIRCUT.

HELPING HANDS!
CATCHING CRIMINALS SHOULD MAKE YOU POPULAR WITH THE POLICE BUT THEY CAN BE FUSSY ABOUT SOMETHING CALLED "DUE PROCESS". WHATEVER THIS IS, IT PROBABLY DOESN'T MATTER.

STYLE MATTERS!
HOW YOU CONDUCT YOUR CRIMEFIGHTING WILL MAKE A DIFFERENCE. BRINGING IN BAD GUYS ALIVE EARNS MORE RESPECT. IF YOUR SUPERHERO NAME IS THE BURGLAR MURDERER, YOU MAY STRUGGLE.

HOLD THE FRONT PAGE!

THE LOCAL NEWSPAPER EDITOR WILL LIKELY BECOME OBSESSED WITH YOU. THIS WILL ALMOST CERTAINLY BE A CRANKY OLD GUY WITH A MOUSTACHE AND A CIGAR.

GIVE 'EM WHAT THEY WANT! YOU CAN GAIN FAVOUR WITH THE EDITOR BY SELLING HIM PHOTOS OF YOUR HERO EXPLOITS, OR EVEN WRITING ABOUT THEM. DON'T WORRY – FOR SOME REASON, HE WILL NEVER FIGURE OUT THAT IT'S YOU.

HER❤ES AND
HEART BREAK

You're going to have to stand up a lot of dates to pursue your crimefighting career, so use our handy excuses to slope off successfully!

RESULTS GUARANTEED!*

"I'VE MADE A HORRIBLE ACCIDENT IN MY PANTS"

"I'VE JUST REMEMBERED, I'M ALLERGIC TO CHAIRS"

"I AM MICK JAGGER AND HAVE FORGOTTEN I'M DUE ON STAGE IN TOKYO IN THREE MINUTES"

"AAARGH! WHO ARE YOU? WHY AM I HERE?"

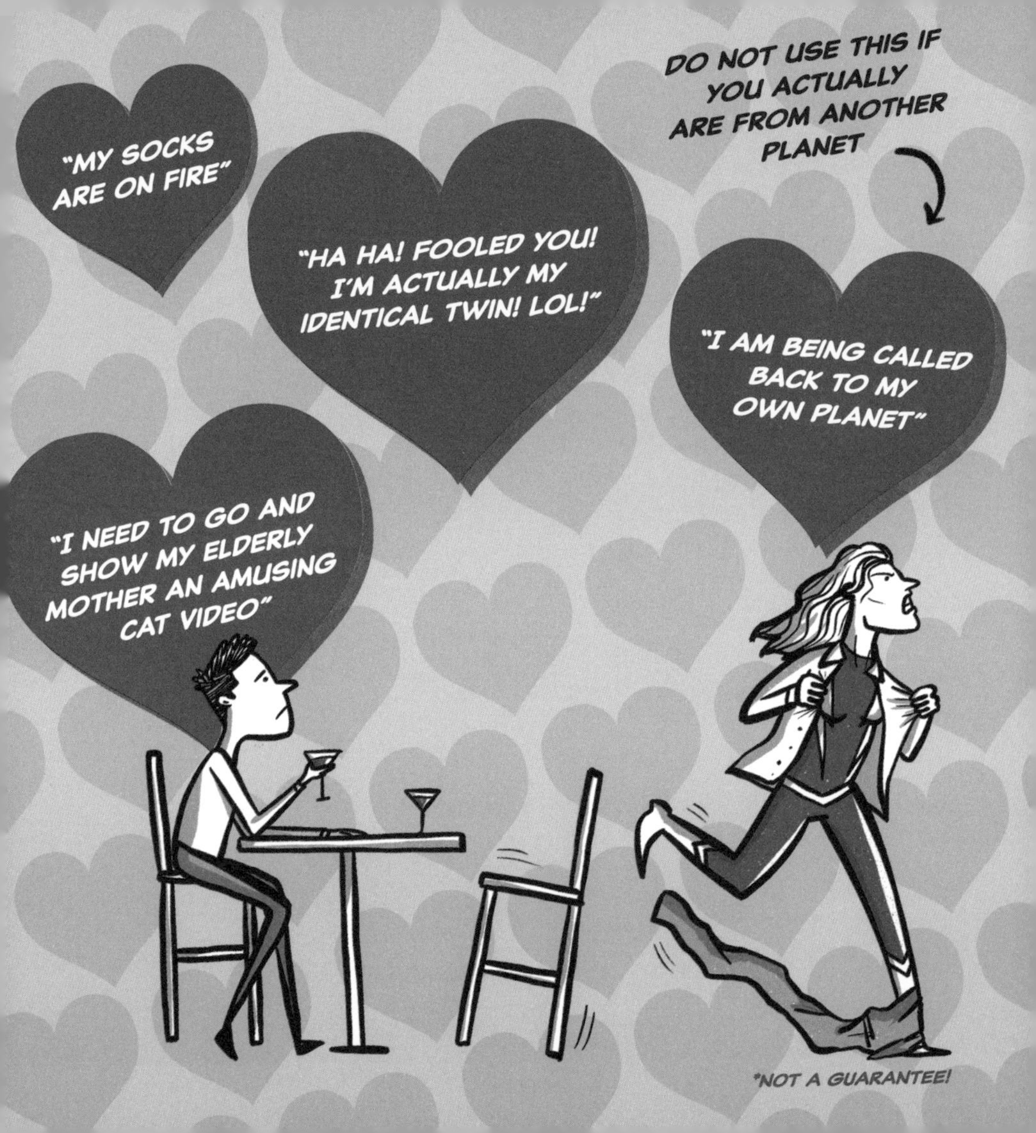
"MY SOCKS ARE ON FIRE"
"HA HA! FOOLED YOU! I'M ACTUALLY MY IDENTICAL TWIN! LOL!"
DO NOT USE THIS IF YOU ACTUALLY ARE FROM ANOTHER PLANET
"I AM BEING CALLED BACK TO MY OWN PLANET"
"I NEED TO GO AND SHOW MY ELDERLY MOTHER AN AMUSING CAT VIDEO"
*NOT A GUARANTEE!

THE SIDE KICK

Do you really need a young hero by your side? Let's weigh up the pros and cons...

CONUNDRUM

YES!
YOU GET TO GIVE THEM CUTE NAMES LIKE BROCCOLI LASS AND KID WINDSOCK!

NO!
THEY KEEP COMING UP WITH CHEESY CATCHPHRASES AND WON'T STOP TEXTING THEIR MATES!

YES!
YOU CAN DRESS THEM IN BRIGHT COLOURS TO DRAW ENEMY FIRE AWAY FROM YOU!

NO!
ISN'T IT ILLEGAL TO USE CHILDREN AS HUMAN SHIELDS IN A WAR AGAINST CRIME?

YES!
THEY'RE EASILY REPLACEABLE – ALTHOUGH ORPHANAGES WILL START TO ASK QUESTIONS AFTER THE FIRST TWO OR THREE!

NO!
THE ONES THAT SURVIVE WILL ALMOST CERTAINLY GROW UP TO BECOME YOUR GREATEST ENEMY!

B

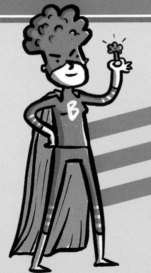

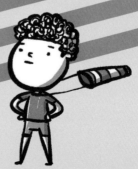

KNOW YOUR NEMESIS

Eventually you're going to find yourself with an arch-enemy. Here's how to recognise them.

MIRROR IMAGE

YOUR NEMESIS WILL OFTEN HAVE OPPOSITE POWERS TO YOU. GOOD AND EVIL. CHAOS AND ORDER. CHALK AND CHEESE. WATCH OUT FOR VILLAINS WITH CHEESE POWERS, BASICALLY.

HAIR RAISER

DO THEY LOOK EXACTLY LIKE YOU BUT HAVE A GOATEE BEARD? PROBABLY TIME TO GET READY FOR A SCRAP.

COPYCATS

ARCH-ENEMIES ARE OBSESSED WITH YOU AND LOVE TO USE CLICHÉS. IF THEY SAY "WE ARE MUCH ALIKE, YOU AND I" IT'S DEFINITELY THEM.

FAMILY FEUD

THERE'S A GOOD CHANCE YOUR NEMESIS WILL BE A SUPER-POWERED MEMBER OF YOUR OWN FAMILY. IS GRANNY LOOKING AT YOU FUNNY? IT'S PROBABLY HER.

AMBITION

YOUR ADVERSARY WON'T THINK SMALL. IF THERE'S ANYONE IN YOUR SOCIAL CIRCLE ALWAYS CHASING A PROMOTION, OR TALKING ABOUT RULING THE GALAXY, PUNCH THEM INTO SPACE JUST TO BE SURE.

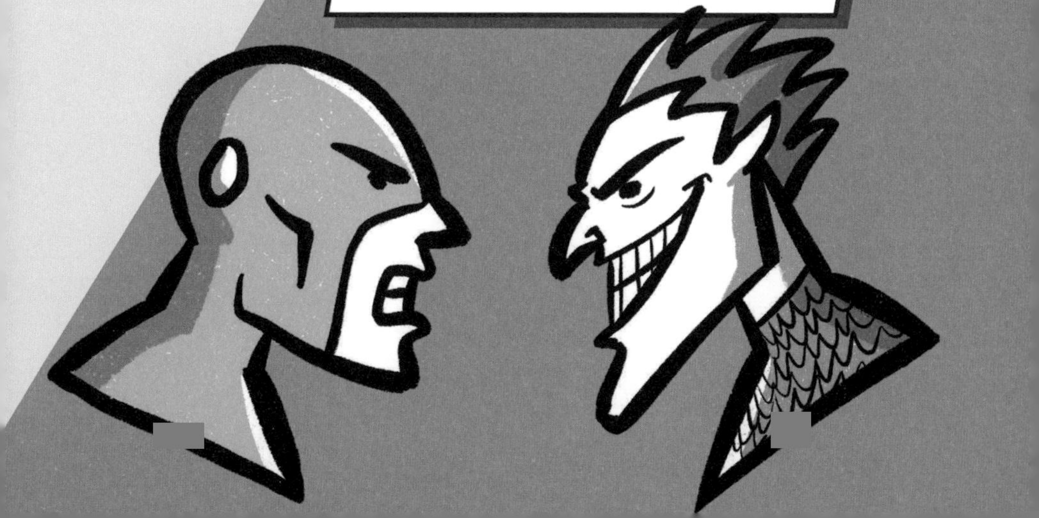

NO T IN TEAM

Etiquette and advice for your first superhero team-up...

DO EXPECT TO FIGHT EACH OTHER BEFORE DECIDING TO WORK TOGETHER. THIS IS AN IMPORTANT TRADITION AND SHOULD NOT BE A SURPRISE.

DON'T FORGET TO COLOUR COORDINATE YOUR COSTUMES BEFORE MEETING UP. NOBODY LIKES A GARISH PINK AND LIME GREEN SUPER-TEAM.

DO MAKE SURE NOBODY HAS SECRET INFORMATION ABOUT THE MURDER OF SOMEBODY ELSE'S PARENTS OR HAVE MOTHERS WHO SHARE THE SAME NAME. TRUST US, THAT SORT OF THING CAN CAUSE BIG PROBLEMS IN THE FUTURE.

DON'T LEAP INTO ACTION WITHOUT DECIDING ON A COOL TEAM NAME, OTHERWISE YOU'LL END UP BEING KNOWN AS THOSE GUYS OVER THERE IN TIGHTS.

DO AGREE IN ADVANCE HOW YOU'RE GOING TO SPLIT THE BILL AFTER YOUR CELEBRATORY VICTORY MEAL. ARGUING OVER STARTERS IS A BAD LOOK FOR HEROES.

DON'T TEAM UP WITH HEROES WHOSE POWERS ARE THE SAME AS YOURS. FIVE PEOPLE WHO CAN CONTROL GRAVY WITH THE POWER OF THEIR MIND ISN'T MUCH MORE USEFUL THAN ONE.

KNOW
your
WEAKNESS

Every hero has a unique vulnerability.
Here's how to stay safe.

GAS ATTACK!
CONTRARY TO POPULAR BELIEF,
GLUTEN IS NOT USUALLY A SUPERHERO
WEAKNESS. YOU MAY JUST HAVE IBS.
CONSULT A DOCTOR AND MAKE SURE
YOUR COSTUME IS WELL VENTILATED.

DEAD OBVIOUS
BULLETS, KNIVES AND
EXPLOSIONS DON'T COUNT.
EVERYBODY IS ALLERGIC
TO THOSE.

OPPOSITES DON'T ATTRACT
YOUR WEAKNESS MAY WELL BE THE OPPOSITE OF YOUR POWERS. IF YOU HAVE FIRE ABILITIES, WATER IS YOUR WEAKNESS. IF YOU HAVE SALT POWERS, STEER CLEAR OF PEPPER. AND SO ON.

ROCK OUT
87% OF SUPERHERO WEAKNESSES ARE CONNECTED TO GLOWING SPACE ROCKS. ANNOYINGLY, 64% OF ALL SUPERPOWERS ALSO COME FROM TOUCHING GLOWING SPACE ROCKS. IT'S A REAL PROBLEM.

87%
64%

ONLY HUMAN
HAVING A WEAKNESS FOR TRIPLE FUDGE CHEESECAKE IS TOTALLY UNDERSTANDABLE. DON'T FIGHT IT.

THE COSMOS AWAITS

You can only fight crime in the streets for so long. Sooner or later, every superhero ends up in outer space and alternate dimensions...

DRESS ACCORDINGLY

YOU'RE GOING TO NEED A FANCY NEW COSTUME WHEN YOU TRAVEL BEYOND OUR REALITY, SO GET A HEAD START AND BEGIN PUTTING IT TOGETHER NOW. JUST MAKE SURE IT'S AIRTIGHT.

BE PREPARED

YES, ALIENS EXIST. THEY WILL PROBABLY TRY TO KILL YOU. ALSO, FOR SOME REASON, THERE ARE PLANETS AND DIMENSIONS FULL OF EARTH ANIMALS THAT CAN TALK. JUST GO WITH IT.

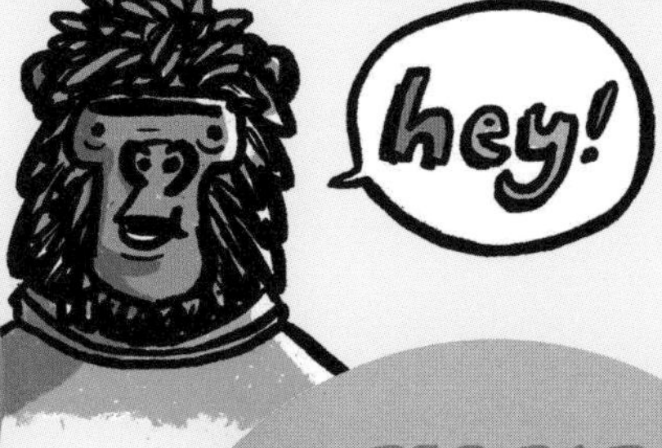
hey!

BIG BAD

EVERY DIMENSION OR GALAXY HAS AN ULTIMATE BAD GUY. HE'LL PROBABLY BE BLUE OR PURPLE, AT LEAST 7 FEET TALL AND HAVE A NAME THAT SOUNDS LIKE BRAXOX OR THRUMCRAX. KEEP YOUR EYES OPEN.

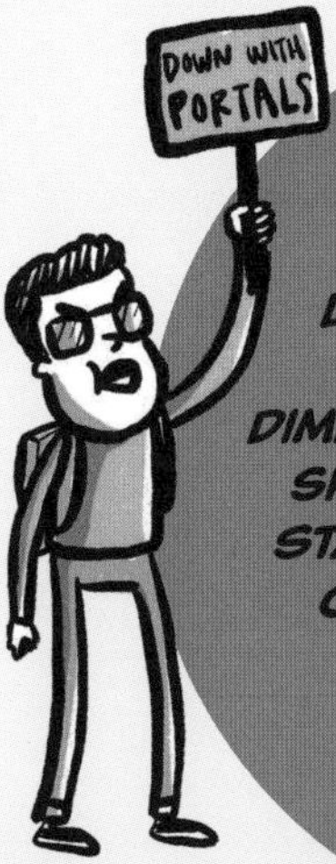
DOWN WITH PORTALS

BORDER CONTROL

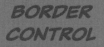

LITERALLY EVERY ALIEN INVASION INVOLVES A DIMENSIONAL PORTAL IN THE SKY OVER A MAJOR CITY. START PETITIONING LOCAL GOVERNMENT NOW TO CRACK DOWN ON THESE HAZARDOUS INTERGALACTIC LOOPHOLES.

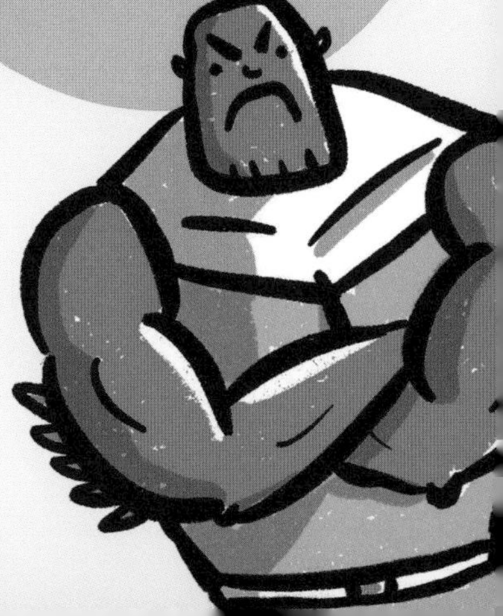

DRESS FOR THE OCCASION

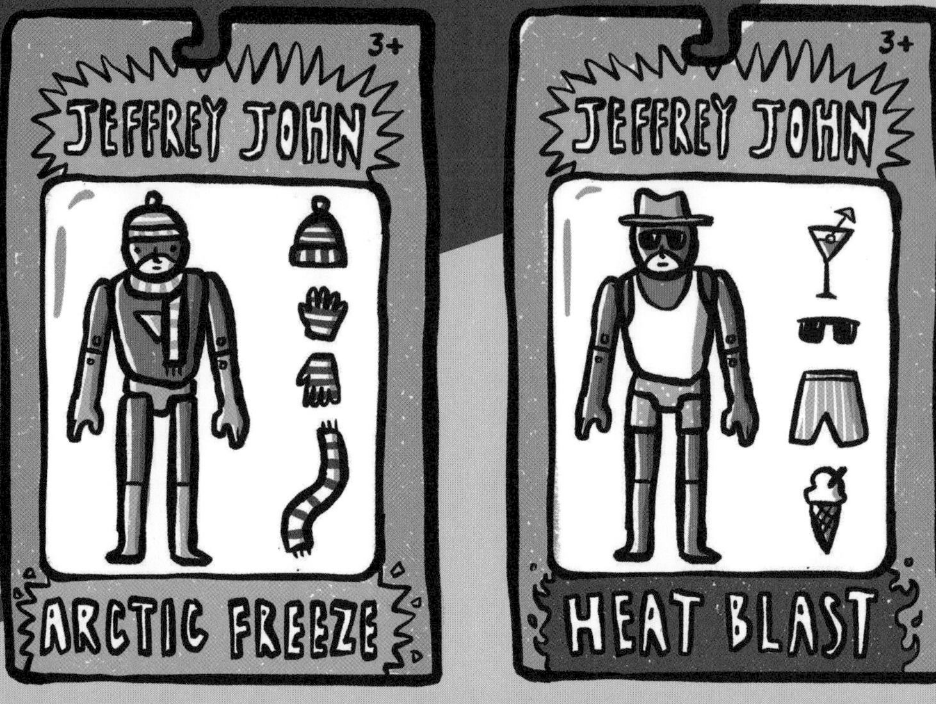
3+
JEFFREY JOHN
ARCTIC FREEZE
3+
JEFFREY JOHN
HEAT BLAST

A variety of costumes means you're ready for any situation, but also means more action figures! Ka-ching!

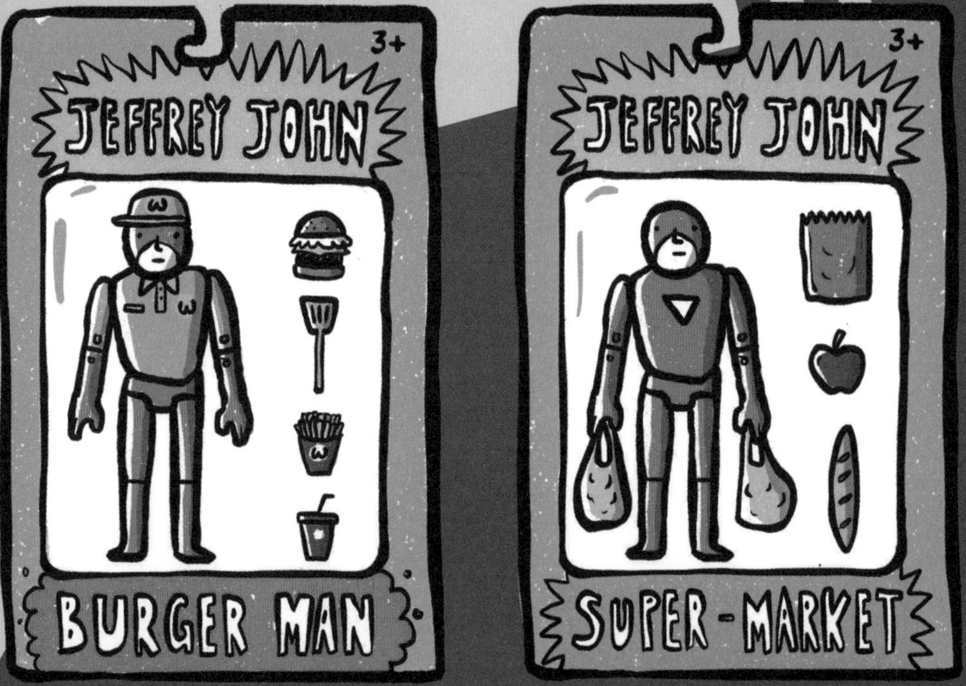
3+
JEFFREY JOHN
BURGER MAN
3+
JEFFREY JOHN
SUPER-MARKET

THE AGE OF HEROES

Hitting middle age doesn't mean you have to give up your hero work. You just need to make a few changes...

DON'T RELY ON BEING A SILENT AVENGER ANY MORE. CRIMINALS WILL HEAR THE CREAKING AND CRACKING OF YOUR KNEES LONG BEFORE YOU'RE IN STRIKING DISTANCE.

DO CONSIDER TACKLING MORE CRIMES DURING THE DAYTIME. THAT WAY YOU CAN FALL ASLEEP ON THE SOFA BY 10PM WITHOUT FEELING GUILTY.

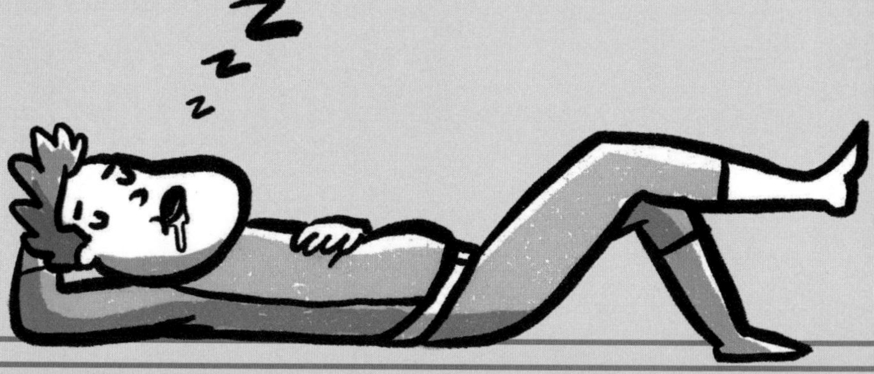
Z
Z
Z

DON'T SPEND TOO MUCH TIME PROWLING THE ROOFTOPS ON PATROL. THERE ARE NO TOILETS UP THERE, AND YOU NOW HAVE A BLADDER THE SIZE OF A WALNUT.

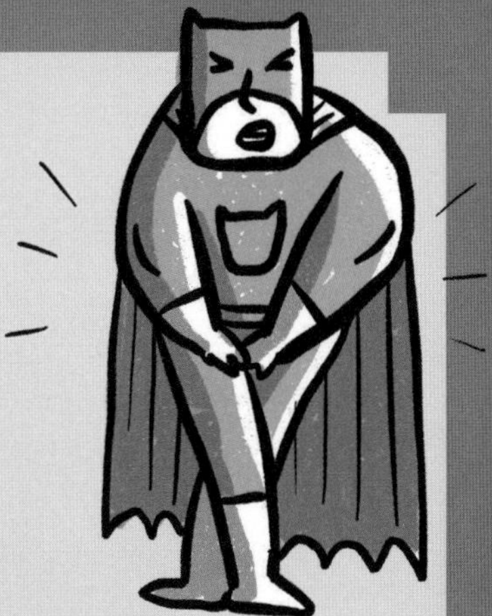

DO ACCEPT THAT BOTH CRIMINALS AND POLICE WILL INCREASINGLY LOOK LIKE SCHOOL CHILDREN AND WILL ALMOST CERTAINLY START USING SLANG THAT YOU WILL NEVER EVER UNDERSTAND. THIS IS FINE.

DON'T BE AFRAID TO UPDATE YOUR TECHNOLOGY. A FOUR-DOOR HATCHBACK HERO MOBILE IS PERFECTLY SENSIBLE AND MORE FUEL EFFICIENT DURING LONG TRIPS.

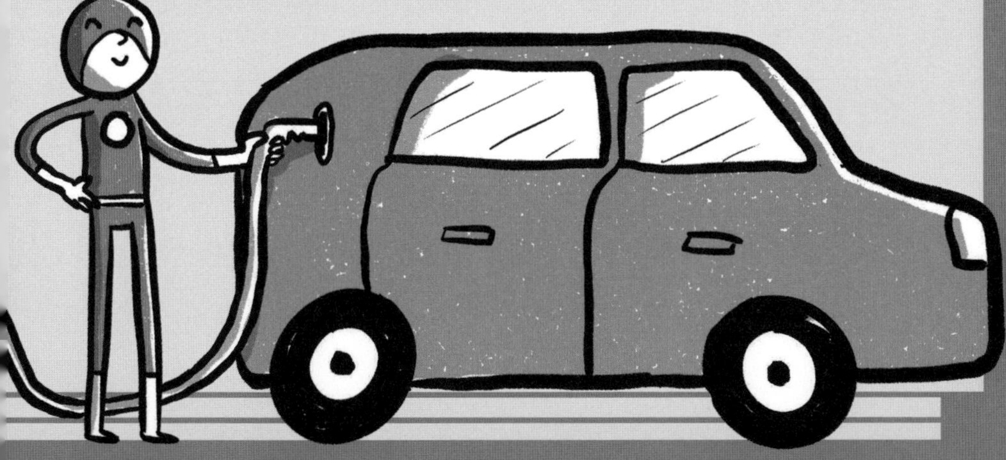

Nothing gets attention like a dramatic exit and every hero should know when to quit...

SUPERHERO
NO MORE

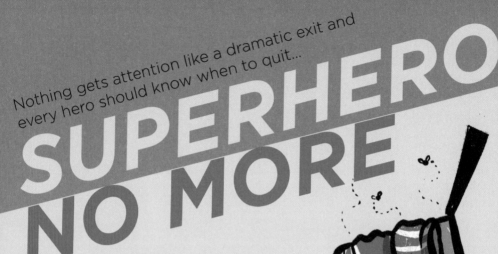

JUST STOP!

THIS IS THE EASIEST METHOD, AND SIMPLY REQUIRES YOU TO THROW YOUR COSTUME INTO THE TRASH AND WALK AWAY SOLEMNLY. FOR SOME REASON, THIS WORKS EVEN BETTER IF THERE'S NOBODY THERE TO SEE IT.

TAKE A BREAK!

LITERALLY! THE BEST EXCUSE FOR HITTING PAUSE ON YOUR HERO CAREER IS TO SUFFER A CATASTROPHIC INJURY AT THE HANDS OF A NEW AND POWERFUL VILLAIN. REQUIRES A CERTAIN AMOUNT OF DEDICATION TO PULL OFF, ALONG WITH A LOT OF PAINKILLERS.

FAKE IT!

ANOTHER OPTION IS TO ABANDON YOUR OLD HERO IDENTITY AND TAKE ON A COMPLETELY NEW ONE. JUST BE SURE NOBODY CAN CONNECT THE TWO. IF CAPTAIN OWL VANISHES, BUT A NEW HERO CALLED THE HOOTER APPEARS, YOU'RE NOT FOOLING ANYONE.

I'LL BE BACK!

OF COURSE, YOU'RE NOT RETIRING FOR GOOD! LEAVE IT A FEW MONTHS AND STAGE YOUR "SURPRISE" COMEBACK! JUST REMEMBER TO GIVE THE OLD COSTUME A WASH FIRST.

PREPARE FOR STARDOM

You've made it! They're going to make a movie about your adventures, so here's what to expect...

YOU WILL ALMOST CERTAINLY BE PLAYED BY A HUNKY BLOND MAN CALLED CHRIS. YES, EVEN IF YOU'RE A WOMAN. SORRY, THAT'S JUST HOW IT WORKS.

YOU WON'T BE ALLOWED TO HAVE THE LIMELIGHT TO YOURSELF. YOUR MOVIE WILL BE USED TO INTRODUCE AT LEAST FIFTEEN OTHER CHARACTERS, WHO WILL ALL GET THEIR OWN MOVIES AS WELL.

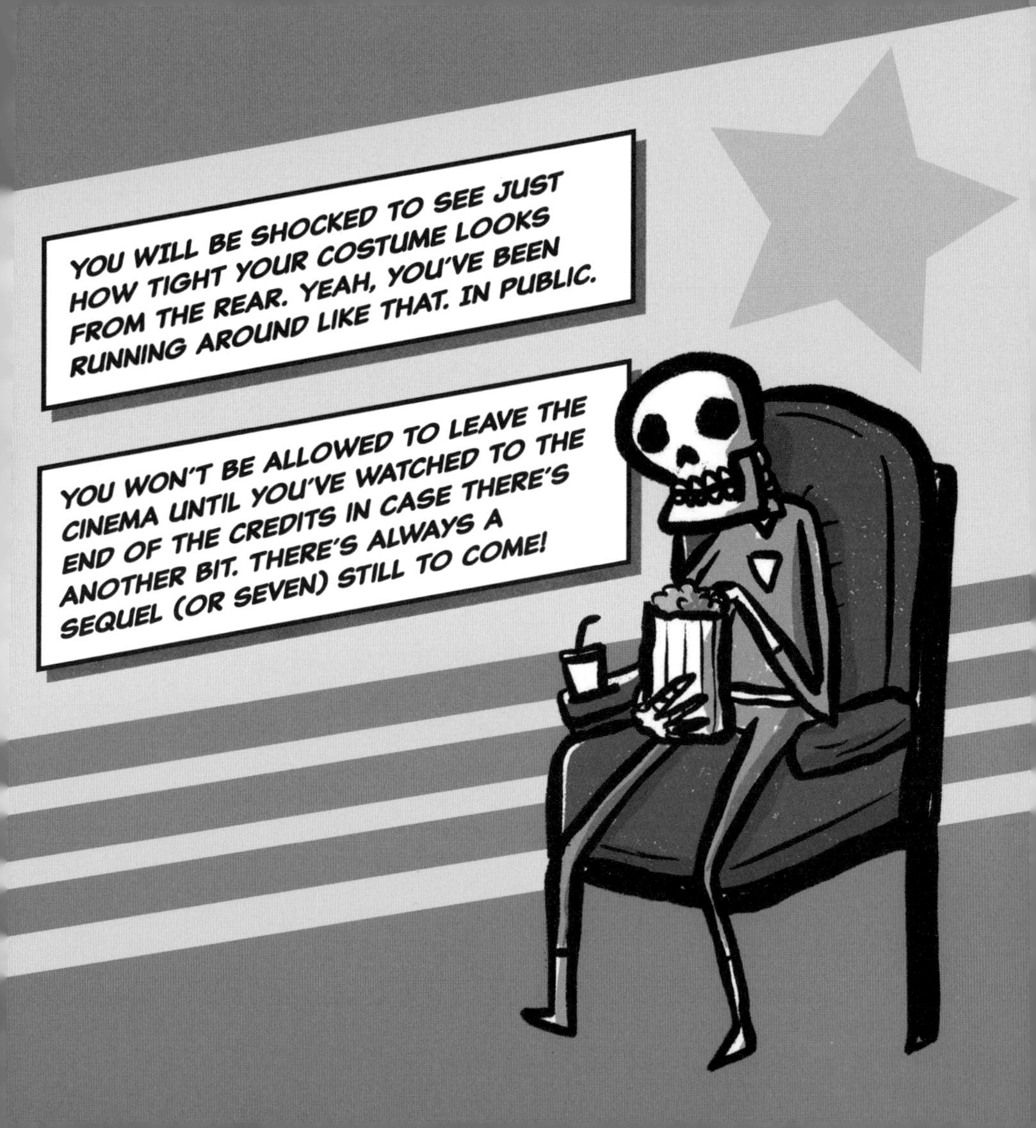
YOU WILL BE SHOCKED TO SEE JUST HOW TIGHT YOUR COSTUME LOOKS FROM THE REAR. YEAH, YOU'VE BEEN RUNNING AROUND LIKE THAT. IN PUBLIC.
YOU WON'T BE ALLOWED TO LEAVE THE CINEMA UNTIL YOU'VE WATCHED TO THE END OF THE CREDITS IN CASE THERE'S ANOTHER BIT. THERE'S ALWAYS A SEQUEL (OR SEVEN) STILL TO COME!

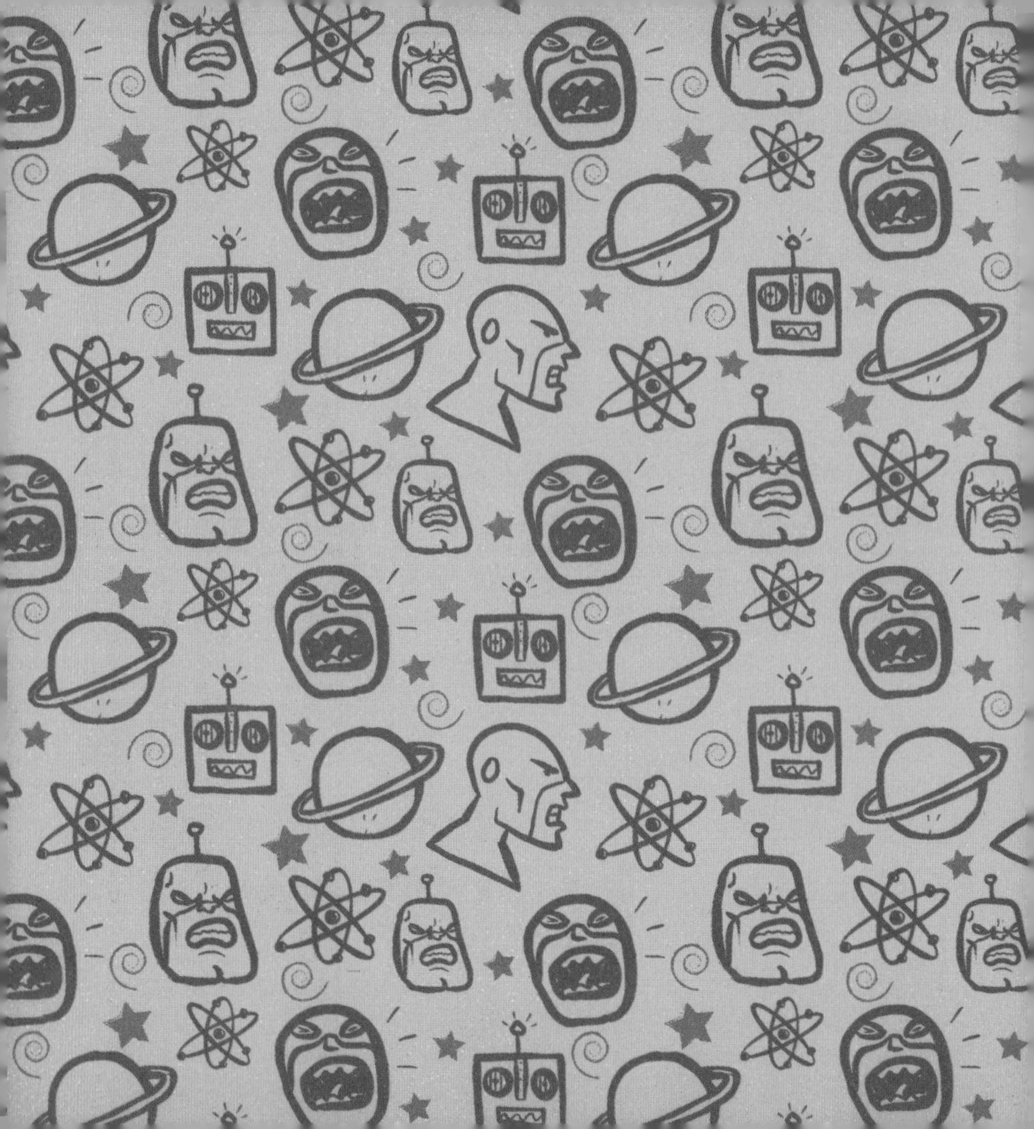